D0200848

my favorite plant

my favorite plant

EDITED AND WITH AN INTRODUCTION BY

Jamaica
KINCAID

Writers and Gardeners on the Plants They Love

FARRAR, STRAUS AND GIROUX

NEW YORK

FARRAR, STRAUS AND GIROUX

19 UNION SQUARE WEST, NEW YORK 10003

Library of Congress Cataloging-in-Publication Data
My favorite plant: writers and gardeners on the plants they love/
edited and with an introduction by Jamaica Kincaid.—1st ed.
        p.   cm.
    ISBN 0-374-28193-9 (alk. paper)
    1. Gardening—Anecdotes.   2. Gardeners—Anecdotes.   3. Authors—
Anecdotes.   4. Flowers—Anecdotes.   5. Plants, Cultivated—
Anecdotes.   I. Kincaid, Jamaica.
SB455.M9   1998   98-22779
635—dc21

ACKNOWLEDGMENTS

A CONCERTED EFFORT HAS BEEN MADE TO CONTACT
THE RIGHTS HOLDERS OF COPYRIGHTED WORKS.
GRATEFUL ACKNOWLEDGMENT IS MADE TO THE FOLLOWING:

"Buds," from *The Gardener's Year*, by Karel Čapek. The Czech original was published in Prague in 1929. The English translation, by M. and R. Weatherall, was first published in Great Britain in 1931 by George Allen & Unwin Ltd.

"A Day on the Edge of the World," from *Plant Hunting on the Edge of the World*, by F. Kingdon Ward, copyright © 1930 by the Estate of F. Kingdon Ward. Reprinted by permission of The Peters Fraser and Dunlop Group Limited on behalf of: The Estate of Frank Kingdon Ward.

"Purple Anemones" and "Sicilian Cyclamens" by D. H. Lawrence, edited by V. De Sola Pinto & F. W. Roberts, from *The Complete Poems of D. H. Lawrence*, edited by V. De Sola Pinto & F. W. Roberts. Copyright © 1964, 1971 by Angelo Ravagli and C. M. Weekley, executors of the Estate of Frieda Lawrence Ravagli. Used by permission of Viking Penguin, a division of Penguin Putnam Inc.

For Elaine
    and
For Philip
    with Love,
        A Garden!

CONTENTS

INTRODUCTION

I AM AMAZED AT SUCH A THING: THAT I would have asked writers who have a garden, writers whom I admire who do not have a garden but have a passion or a memory of some kind about flowers, writers who are gardeners and write about it with all its ups and downs, its disappointments, its rewards, and who are attached to the garden with a blindness, plus a jumble of feelings that mere language (as far as I can see) seems inadequate to express, or to define an attachment that is so ordinary: to a plant, loved especially for something endemic to it (it cannot help its situation: it loves the wet, it loves the dry, it reminds the person seeing it of a wave or a waterfall or some event that contains so personal an experience such as: when my mother would not allow me to do something I particularly wanted to do, and in my misery I noticed that the frangipani tree was in bloom).

I know gardeners well (or at least I think I do, for I am a gardener, too, but I experience it as an act of utter futility, I shall never have the garden I have in my mind, but that for me is the joy of it; certain things can never be realized and so all the

more reason to attempt them). I know their fickle-
ness, I know their weakness for wanting in their
own gardens the thing they have never seen before,
or never possessed before, or saw in a garden (their
friends') something which they do not have and
would like to have (though what they really like and
envy—especially that, envy—is the entire garden they
are seeing, but as a disguise they focus on just one
thing: the Mexican poppies, the giant butterbur,
the extremely plump blooms of white, purple,
black, pink, green hellebores emerging from the
cold, damp, and brown earth).

I was not surprised that everyone I asked had
something definite that they liked. Gardeners (or
just plain simple writers who write about the garden) always have something they like intensely and
in particular, right at the moment you engage them
in the reality of the borders they cultivate, the space in
the garden they occupy; at any moment, they like
in particular this, or they like in particular that.
Nothing in front of them (that is, in the borders
they cultivate, the space in the garden they occupy)
is repulsive and fills them with hatred, or this thing

would not be in front of them. They only love, and they only love in the moment; when the moment has passed they love the memory of the moment, they love the memory of that particular plant or that particular bloom, but the plant of the bloom itself, they have moved on from; they have left it behind for something else, something new, especially something from far away, and from so far away, a place they will never live (occupy, cultivate; the Himalayas, just for an example).

Of all the benefits that come from having endured childhood (for it is something to which we must submit, no matter how beautiful we find it, no matter how enjoyable it has been) certainly among them will be the garden and the desire to be involved with gardening. A gardener's grandmother will have grown such and such a rose, and the smell of that rose at dusk (for flowers always seem to be most smelling at the end of the day, as if that, smelling, was the last thing to do before going to sleep), when the gardener was a child and walking in that grandmother's footsteps as she went about her business in her garden—the memory of that smell of the rose combined with the memory of that smell of the grandmother's skirt will forever inform and influence the life of the gardener, inside or outside the garden itself. And so in a conversation with such a person (a gardener), a sentence, a thought that goes something like this—"You know when I was such and such an age, I went to the market for a reason that is no longer of any particular interest to me, but it was there I saw for the first time something that I have never and can never forget"—floats out into the clear air, and the person from whom these words or this thought emanates is standing in front of you all bare and trembly, full of feeling, full of memory. Memory is a gardener's real palette; memory as it summons up the past, memory as it shapes the present, memory as it dictates the future.

This book, this anthology, this collection of essays that you (a reader) hold in your hands is meant to be like a garden, a garden that I might make, for everything in it, every flower, every tree, every whatever enclosed here, everything mentioned has made a claim on my memory and passion at some moment in my life as a gardener. I have never been able to grow *Meconopsis betonicifolia* with success (it sits there, a green rosette of leaves, looking at me with no bloom. I look back at it myself, without a pleasing countenance), but the picture of it that I have in my mind, a picture made up of memory (I saw it some time ago), a picture made up of "to come" (the future, which is the opposite of remembering), is so intense that whatever happens between me and this plant will never satisfy the picture I have of it (the past remembered, the past to come). I first saw it (*Meconopsis betonicifolia*) in Wayne Winterrowd's garden (a garden he shares with that other garden eminence Joe Eck), and I shall never see this plant (in flower or not, in the wild or cultivated) again without thinking of him (of them, really—he and Joe Eck) and saying to myself, It shall never look quite like this (the way I saw it in their garden), for in their garden it was itself and beyond comparison (whatever that should amount to right now, whatever that might ultimately turn out to be), and I will always want it to look that way, growing comfortably in the mountains of Vermont, so far away from the place to which it is endemic, so far away from the place in which it was natural, un-noticed, and so going about its own peculiar ways of perpetuating itself (perennial, biannual, mono-carpic or not).

What I mean to say in the end is that this book, this collection of essays, looks to me like a land-scape, an enclosure, a garden I would create, if I could. The ideal garden that I would make begins with Wayne (Winterrowd) and ends with Elaine (Scarry). I first came to the garden with practicality in mind, a real beginning which would lead to a real end: where to get this, how to grow that. Where to get this was always nearby, a nursery never too far away; how to grow that led me to acquire volume upon volume, books all with the same advice (likes shade, does not tolerate lime, needs staking), but in the end I came to know how to grow the things I like to grow through looking—at other people's gar-dens. I imagine they acquired knowledge of such things in much the same way—looking and looking at somebody else's garden.

But about this book again: I have tried to

arrange these essays and poems (and excerpts from gardeners, be they in the wild like Frank Kingdon Ward in the foothills of the Himalayas, or at home like Katharine S. White on a farm in Maine) in such a way as to give the illusion of a garden, a garden I would like (*sometimes, only sometimes, feelings about a garden will change, too*), a garden of words and images made of words, and flowers turned into words, and the words in turn making the flower, the plant, the bean (Maxine Kumin) visible. I loved reading all the pieces in here. I was amazed by and grateful for the generosity of the contributors, but then gardeners will give wholeheartedly and bigheartedly; that is why they are allowed to covet. At the end of it (this book), I hope the reader will have some satisfaction—not complete satisfaction, only some satisfaction. A garden, no matter how good it is, must never completely satisfy. The world as we know it, after all, began in a very good garden, a completely satisfying garden—Paradise—but after a while the owner and the occupants wanted more.

Jamaica Kincaid
Vermont, March 1998

Plant name conventions have changed over time, and may even vary from writer to writer. Standard practice today is to put Latin names in italics and cultivar names in single quotation marks. In *My Favorite Plant*, writers have been edited for consistency within their pieces, but the entire collection has not been edited for conformity to a single style. Similarly, British spelling has not been Americanized.

my favorite plant

MECONOPSIS
by Wayne Winterrowd

ITT HAPPENS OFTEN TO CHILDREN—AND sometimes to gardeners—that they are given gifts the value of which they do not perceive until much later. That is how it was with my first meconopsis. Seventeen years ago, when my garden in Vermont was so young that it was really only a nursery, I visited a very good gardener in New Hampshire. It was spring, and his garden, enviably long-established, was at its peak of vernal beauty. We walked about in that happy conjunction of need and generosity that all gardeners know, I admiring and he digging. My cardboard box was almost full of roots, slips, and young plants when we came to the stream that flows through his garden. He bent over a patch of mousy, furred, upturned gray leaves and said, "This is the very best thing. You have to have it."

It was *Meconopsis betonicifolia*, and he must have wondered why I did not immediately fall to my knees. Maybe he wondered, too, whether my ignorance made a waste of his gift. His instructions (repeated twice, as one does with children) were in any case very clear. "Divide it into single crows with a bit of root when you get home. Plant them firmly just at the crown, like strawberries, in rich decayed leaf mold. Bright dappled light. Maybe some morning sun. But pinch out the first flower bud. You *must* pinch out the first flower bud."

All those first steps were easy, and each single crown caught and flourished in the cool bed I had made them beside my own little stream. The first summer they made foot-wide rosettes of oval, dull-ish blue, hairy leaves, nice enough, but hardly to be treasured like the lusty hosta 'Royal Standard,' or the dusty pink, intensely fragrant *Viola odorata* that had also been in the box. They lived through a cold winter (I was to learn that they love that sort of thing), and the following spring each developing plant clasped a round, fat, furry bud in its center. By then I had discovered something of what I possessed, for I was keyed to the name whenever it appeared in books, as one is when an unfamiliar plant is out in the garden.

I learned that *Meconopsis betonicifolia* is the fabled Himalayan blue poppy (a *blue* poppy: words alone enough to shiver over), that it is to all other garden flowers what a milk-white unicorn might be in a barnyard, and that it is the envy of gardeners the world over. I read in T. H. Everett's *Encyclopedia of Gardening* that "in most parts of America these plants are difficult or impossible to grow," and in *Wyman's Gardening Encyclopedia* that it "always makes a great impression on American tourists, for it is practically unknown in most parts of the U.S." In *The Education of a Gardener*, Russell Page comments that its culture is "as ardently worked for and . . . as difficult to succeed with as the philosopher's stone," and in *Green Thoughts*, Eleanor Perényi whines wistfully that she "would give anything for a glimpse of it, even in somebody else's garden." And there it was, this nonpareil, in thriving health, in *my* garden.

And it was about to bloom there, for the first time. "But pinch out the first flower bud. You *must* . . ." my friend had commented, and there was no ambiguity in his twice-repeated command. As a gardener of fifty years' experience (albeit meconopsisless for all but the last third) I am used to ruthlessness with plants. I can nip out the first hopeful blooms of annuals, and mess up their roots as well, knowing that it will be better for us both later on. I have plunged a butcher's knife into the hearts of magnificent clivias and agapanthus, prying their growth apart with a crunch at their crowns and trimming off their white, fleshy roots as one would cut up servings of baked noodles. I have beheaded ancient lilacs, hoary with lichens, so their youth could return to them. I am inured to these acts of violence, but to pinch out those first buds of *Meconopsis betonicifolia*, when even Eleanor Perényi "would give anything for a glimpse . . ."?

Fortunately, in the nick (so to speak) of time, I met H. Lincoln Foster at a meeting of the Berkshire Chapter of the American Rock Garden Society. Then old and very ill, he was still tending Millstream, his garden in southern Connecticut, and his authority as one of America's greatest gardeners hung about him like a fine, comfortable robe. He explained that meconopsis capable of becoming perennials will expend everything, when they are young seedlings or divisions, on their first flower. They then become "monocarpic" (as many of their tribe always are), fading away after bloom like any common biennial foxglove. But if that first flower is pinched out, some (not all) will settle down to form crowns and persist from year to year as true perennials. "So," he said, "if it is really *betonicifolia* that you have" (as opposed to a dozen other names he reeled off, and I was later to learn, of true biennials, which will be that whatever you do) "you had better pinch."

There it was for a second time, delivered with authority beyond question. And though I confess that in life generally, when faced with a choice between immediate, spendthrift pleasure and careful prudence, I have always tended to take the grasshopper's way, still, to have in my garden such a plant, and to know that one gesture of delayed gratification, one tiny painful pinch, would mean years of perenniality, years of returning pleasure . . . years of unweening pride and smug superiority and the most heartfelt sadness at the bad fortunes of other gardeners . . . well, I pinched. I even smothered down the waffling thought that as I had five plants, perhaps then I could pinch only four, and from one at least see this glory straightaway, though I cost it its life.

It is lucky that I began with *Meconopsis betonicifolia*, because within its genus of about forty-five species, it is the easiest to grow and, when forced to it, the most reliably perennial. And though within its family three or four first cousins vie with it for the title, it is arguably the most beautiful. In its second spring after pinching, it will produce several knots of growth from a central crown, most of which form buds and eventually flowers on stems 4 feet high. Each stem is crowned with one magnificent nodding bloom about 3 inches across, and two to four smaller ones lower down the stem. Petals are usually four, though quite curiously, cultivated plants may bear flowers with six or more petals, a phenomenon never reported in the wild. True doubling, however, seems never to occur, and that is a good thing, as there is a grace about the carriage of the flowers, an almost Tanagra figurine poise, that would only be ruined by too much heavy petal.

Those who can grow the plant at all are quite

snobbish about the color, which at its very best is a clear sky blue almost impossible to imagine when not standing before it. Either because of the provenance of collected seed, however, or—as some speculate—because of the alkalinity or dryness of the soil in which they are grown, plants can produce flowers in a range of color from weaker, more watered blue to mauve and even light brownish-purple. A perfectly blue flower is, one supposes, to be preferred over any other; but in fact, there are no ugly *Meconopsis betonicifolia*, and those that veer furthest from the purest tint do so by washes of one color over another, creating, in their own way, a curious effect of translucence. I even grew—from seed collected by Dan Hinkley on an expedition to Nepal three years ago—a single plant with flowers of deep grape purple. Alas, that one I didn't pinch, and I still wonder whether it might have been the only one of its color ever brought to the Western world or, indeed, the only one that ever existed at all.

For a plant of such celebrity, *Meconopsis betonicifolia* is of surprisingly recent introduction, having been brought to England as seed by Frank Kingdon-Ward from western China in 1924. Graham Stuart Thomas flowered it in his Cambridge garden in 1927, when still, as he says, "a schoolboy" ("It thrilled me beyond measure"). Except for its relatively greater perenniality and its ease of division and increase, it is difficult to explain why it has become *the* Himalayan blue poppy in most people's minds, crowding out *M. grandis*, which ought to have at least an equal share in its distinctions. In the privileged gardens where perennial meconopsis thrive at all, it is the elder, having been brought to the Royal Botanic Garden in Edinburgh as early as 1895, though the first flowers it produced there were a disappointment, described as a "dull portish-red," very bad form indeed for a meconopsis. Later introductions from Sikkim provided flowers of the correct, splendid satin blue, carried, as Graham Stuart Thomas has remarked, "like lampshades" atop sturdy, 4-foot stems. Given the conditions that all meconopsis require—deep leaf-moldy soil, abundant moisture at the roots and in the air, perfect drainage, protection from scorching sun and drying wind, and, most of all, cool summer nights and brisk, buoyant days—M. grandis can settle down to become reliable perennials, easily divided and replanted just as the leaves show in spring. Given these conditions, huge drifts might be built up. And when in bloom, there would be nothing else to look at.

M. grandis will also freely intermarry with *M. betonicifolia*, producing plants of hybrid vigor and splendid flower color. Progeny from these matings are all grouped under the name *Meconopsis × sheldonii*, commemorating a Mr. Sheldon of Oxted, Surrey, the first to think of getting the pair together. Scottish, Irish, and northern English gardeners (who can turn meconopsis tricks with their left hands) rave over some of these crosses, such as 'Branklyn,' the most vigorous and the tallest of the group, with flowers—saucers, rather—as much as 8 inches across. But the crown of beauty goes to 'Slieve Donard,' named after that famous nursery, which is lower in stature and smaller in flower, a good thing, really, as a meconopsis is not a dahlia. For the beauty of its flowers, words run out. A gasp and a wave of the hand must do.

There are other famous crosses between *M. grandis* and *M. betonicifolia*—'Sherriff No. 600,' 'Quarriston,' 'Archie Campbell,' 'Springhill,' and Mrs. Crewdson's 1940 Crewdson's Hybrids—and they are all names to conjure with in the right circles. There is a thrill to be had in visiting the Royal Botanic Garden at Edinburgh at just the right time, when their flowering overlaps. There they are all carefully segregated, but still it would be like running into Helen of Troy, Cleopatra, Antinoüs, and the young Marlon Brando on the same street. As all these hybrids must be increased by patient division of their furry crowns in early spring, only eight nurseries in the United Kingdom list them at all, and two ('Branklyn' and 'Springhill') are to be gotten, if at all, from only one, Ballyrogan Nurseries in Northern Ireland ("by appointment"). Whether they exist in American gardens (which is to say the Pacific Northwest, a sort of meconopsis heaven) I can't say. Certainly they don't grow in

Vermont (which is to the Pacific Northwest something like the Plaza to Heaven), not just yet. But when next I find myself in Northern Ireland, near The Grange, Ballyrogan, Newtownards, C. Down, N.I. BT23 45D, then I mean to try. Meanwhile, I am content with my one *Meconopsis × sheldonii*, which, though a good deep blue—actually what one could call a *neon* blue—might still nod its head even lower before 'Branklyn' or 'Slieve Donard.'

Not all meconopsis are some shade of blue (pure or imperfect) and not all are terribly difficult to grow. By far the easiest is *Meconopsis cambrica*, the Welsh poppy, which is actually a beautiful plant, though its cheerful colors—citron yellow or orange—and its amiable nature have put it at a disadvantage in its haughty clan. Though generally listed as hardy from zones 9 to 6, it is much sturdier than that, surviving and self-seeding pleasantly here in Vermont. It is the only member of its genus native to Western Europe, and before the introduction of Asian species, its status was a little higher than that of the poor relation it has now. From furred, bright green, 8-inch leaves, many hairy stems arise, each surmounted by a single, nodding bud that splits in half to shake out a crinkled, 2-inch-wide flower. Like most poppies and many anemones, it is a flower of the wind, the slightest breeze causing it to dance, until it drops its petals, in three or four days, to form seed capsules. Unlike its treasured Asian relatives (seed of which must be sown in autumn and carried over the winter with never a check), *M. cambrica* germinates freely in the garden, so much so that in gardens it really likes, it can become a nuisance. But because of its great charm, it is never such a terrible nuisance. It is easy to grub it out where it is not wanted (it hates, like all *Papaveraceae*, any disturbance at its roots), and it is often a pleasant surprise to find it poking out of some place where it was not planted. The species is a clear yellow, though the orange variety, 'Aurantiaca,' seems so much in its blood that a nice mix of lemons and oranges together will generally occur. There is as well a double-flowered form, 'Flore Pleno,' that is nice all by itself, but not mixed with the singles, because then it makes them look as if something is missing.

One other group of meconopsis demands attention from those gardeners who can grow them, not for their flowers, but for their leaves. The love of leaves is perhaps the most refined of gardening pleasures, for most gardeners begin by wanting flowers, and many end up there. Leaves—and their beauty—are, when they are appreciated at all, mere essential accidents on the way to the main thing. It is true that hostas, among usual garden plants, are grown for their foliage, and the flowers, though often quite nice (at least at first), are scornfully clipped away. There are plants as well—connoisseur plants to which one comes eventually—that are leaf-proud, such as *Petasites japonicus* var. *giganteus*, the giant Japanese butterbur, or the cream-splashed, oval-leaved *Tovaria virginiana* 'Variegata,' now painfully renamed as part of the genus *Fallopia*. But to grow anything other than a privet or a pachysandra for its leaves alone seems odd to many gardeners. Especially odd in a meconopsis.

Still, both *Meconopsis paniculata* and *M. napaulensis* will stop you dead in your tracks on an autumn stroll through the garden, when they are not in flower and not in blue. That is, they will if you garden where Asian meconopsis thrive and you grow them. Both natives of the high elevations of Nepal and western China, they are inured to life-threatening cold, which they seem almost to require for survival. Their built-in blankets would else go to waste. *M. napaulensis* is thickly fleeced with silver over lettuce-green leaves, and *M. paniculata* with gold over mustard-yellow. Both these meconopsis look heavily armed, but a touch will show that they are as soft as any goose's breast. The spines of cactus make sense, for they are generally protective devices, a sort of *noli me tangere* to would-be molesters. Maybe, as often happens in the animal and plant kingdoms (and with people), a bit of fakery is thought to do for the real thing. Most probably, the hairs are a cunning device to catch dew and raindrops, thus creating a humid microclimate around each plant. Practical as that might be for the plant, it is also a delight to the gardener, for when the foot-wide rosettes of lobed leaves are beaded over, they seem made of glass, the one silver and the other gold.

Both *M. paniculata* and *M. napaulensis* are mono-
carpic, and that is the curse they bear. To be mono-
carpic is not necessarily to be biennial, since,
though some plants will flower the second year
from seed, most will wait two years, or even three,
before thrusting up towering flower stalks in early
June. *M. paniculata* may reach 6 feet, with generally
yellow, pendulous, 2-inch flowers, though pink
forms may occur; *M. napaulensis* can be even taller,
perhaps to 8 feet, with flowers of clear blue, brick
red, pink, purple, and very occasionally white.
Early in their flowering, both possess startling
beauty, but like a few other flowering plants (such
as *Liatris spicata*, the 'Kansas gayfeather') the flowers
open at the top of the stalk and move downward; so
the show, at its middle and end, is somewhat
marred by the passing of the main characters. One
need not look, either, for the beautiful rosette of
leaves, since it will be all withered away, never to return again.

No Asian meconopsis has ever reappeared here
from self-sown seed, presumably because the winters are too cold for their survival. So the fine

grains must be shaken from gaunt stalks, seeded immediately, pricked out, and carried through their first winter in a very cool greenhouse, to be planted out in spring. As with all monocarpic plants, it is a lot of work. But in leaf and in flower, both *M. paniculata* and *M. napaulensis* are so beautiful that it is worth the trouble. Besides, it is another distinction for the garden.

Gardening as I do in a very cold section of the country, where minimum winter lows routinely reach −20° Fahrenheit, and where there are scarcely 100 frost-free days between the last cold snap in spring (May) and the first of autumn (early September), I have had to become inured to more insults than the weather. The worst come from fellow gardeners who live in milder climates and who routinely ask why I have chosen such a place to spend my gardening life, where "as the world knows, little can flourish but lichens." It is always on the surface a well-meant question, rather like "Why do you drink so much?" or "Why have you gotten so stout?" But it hides within it a certain smugness, a tone of self-congratulation born of the conviction that they—from luck, chance, or choice—never have committed such a folly, and never would.

My answers to this question vary with the slant of my interlocutor. For those who care about such things, political, social, and ecological considerations make it easy to justify living in Vermont. Those who can see the beauty of its wooded hills, the purity of its air, the glory of its autumn and its deep, snowy winter silences are also simple to shut up. But the real gardener, the committed crank, still will drone on. "Yes, but what can you *grow*?"

If they are on the spot, they can look about the garden, which now comprises about seven acres, with many plants (such as stewartias, listed to zone 5, or halesias, to zone 6) that might be surprises flourishing here. The climate, for all its brutal winter cold, provides much help in accommodating plants assumed to be too tender for Vermont. Summer droughts are rare, so in July and August lawns remain emerald green. Soils, at least in my part of the state, are very nearly perfect, deep, humus-rich, and free-draining, the proverbial "sandy loam" seldom met with elsewhere. An elevation of about 1,800 feet gives the garden cool nights and bright, warm days, just the conditions that so many garden plants relish. Snow cover is deep and reliable, blanketing the garden in winter in a way that I have come to think of as curiously warm, for all its icy whiteness. And by many tricks and feints, first from necessity and now with odd pleasure, I have become adept at playing games with hardiness, which is, for gardeners located in areas like mine, another sort of outdoor winter sport.

But still, if I had to name—if I were positively required to name—one group of plants I grow that justifies where I garden, it would be meconopsis. How dreadfully sad I am for other gardeners who cannot have them.

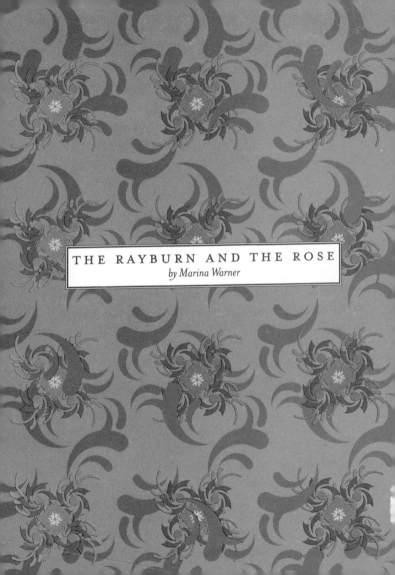

THE RAYBURN AND THE ROSE
by Marina Warner

❁ ❁ ❁ ❁ ❁ ❁ ❁ ❁ ❁ ❁ ❁ ❁ ❁

MY RAMBLING GUINÉE, ONE OF the darkest and muskiest of all roses, has been cut and bent down on its side and bundled in strips of blue kitchen rags (the variety called J-cloths in England); it's now lying shipwrecked athwart the mobcap hydrangea. This was my friend Henrietta's remedy, to save the rose from being mangled when the men came to fell the almond tree in which Guinée was all entwined. The tree, which was here when I first moved into my house, died of old age; the spread and angles of its dark branches marked the end of the cul-de-sac where I live and I used to fancy it turned the street into one of those Chinese scrolls, painted with a swashbuckling ideogram for happiness or long life or good fortune.

Early in the summer, after the almond blossom has long gone, scattering the winter in a gentle sprinkle of pink, Guinée's dark, tender and fat buds would appear, tinged black on each petal's furled edge. When the roses opened, sable shadows welled in between their velvet, with a sheen in its crimson such as the Venetians achieve with translucent glaze upon glaze. I imagine that when this deep deep rose was successfully bred, it was named Guinée by a French nurseryman who had been steeped, as educated Frenchmen are, in Baudelairean dreams of *luxe, calme et volupté,* and he was following a train of associations that leads from the poet's dreamed *Vénus noire,* Jeanne Duval, to the coast of West Africa, that point of departure for so many in the black diaspora. But the name Guinée— guinea—was also used as an insult for Italians during the early waves of immigration to the United States. My mother was born in Puglia in southern Italy, and her whole family left for Chicago in the first decade of the century, only to return, whipped by the American backlash of the twenties. So the passionate darkness of the rose called Guinée connects me to my mother, too.

From my bedroom, in late May, I'd begin to see Guinée's lovely dark heads resting here and there against the lighter spears of the almond's foliage. I'd go down and climb onto the dustbins, which stand incongruously under the almond tree, to pick a rose and bring it in: its scent was alive, and the black-crimson velvet of the petals warm when you stroked them, as I could not help doing. But this sense of the flesh in the rose is still innocent, in spite of the sumptuousness of the flower's colour and fragrance and swirl: touching Guinée recalls the skin of a baby. Its sweet musk is quick and fresh, again like something newly sprung.

The men came yesterday to cut down the dead almond; it was early in the morning, a quiet week-day, everyone in my street already gone to work. We had a quick, deadly row. I was anxious about my tree and my garden and they were young, large louts with big mouths and heavy boots who flung down their tools on the garden, snapping a clematis at the root and trampling the dwarf geranium and the lamb's tongues ground cover as if they'd been let loose on a demolition job on a garage. So I sent them packing and they went, leaving the sere almond still standing, and Guinée bundled up, waiting for a new host. I am considering a Judas tree. Its acid-pink blossom will banish the winter greys with a flourish, and its later, hoofprint-bunched leaves might make an odd but striking setting for the rose's splendour.

When I was twelve, my father planted a rose garden round our family house near Cambridge, where he was a bookseller. The plan stood on the mantelpiece in the drawing room, and it was one of those family jokes that are constantly recalled with fond chuckles that a snobbish friend picked it up and, looking at the diagram of beds with the names filled in—Cécile Brunner, Madame Albert Carrière, Madame Grégoire Staechlin, Albertine, Constance Spry—exclaimed, "Good heavens, Plum (this was my father's nickname), what a bizarre *placement*! What kind of a dinner party is this?" I used to walk around with him when he was proudly showing the growing roses to a visitor. He'd talk about feeding them with bonemeal and blood, of keeping them happy in the heavy fenland clay, of the necessary curbing of their high spirits and the risk of waterlogging in the region's persistent rain-fall—the buds would swell and tarnish on the stem. "Shrouded nuns," he called them. He was reluctant to prune hard, however, and raged, too, against municipal and suburban garden maintenance men, who cut roses back to the root each year. He was filled with enthusiasm for his roses' potential, and he worried that they might be harshly handled, undernourished, blighted; anyone who was employed to help was always dismissed almost immediately. They were his nurslings. I realised, eavesdropping as he hobbyhorsed about his roses, that everything he said about them could be said of us, his two daughters. He had a terrible temper, but he was an indulgent father and did not prune us back. Guinée was his favourite, and it carries his memory vividly for me.

In the raw lightless mornings of the long winter months of East Anglia, he'd go out in his carpet slippers and his worn tweed dressing gown, which, the original belt lost long ago, he tied with a tasselled curtain pull. He'd take the path beside the rose garden to the coal hole and we'd hear the scrape of the shovel and the tumble of the coal into the scuttle; he'd return to the kitchen, where my mother would be at the Rayburn, riddling the grate with an ingenious hooked poker in order to rekindle the embers of the night, and then raking the spent clinkers and ashes into the pan. Afterwards, she'd mop the floor and wipe the woolly brickdust such a stove exhales onto every surface and into every cranny.

There was no central heating in the house—as was common in England until twenty years ago. The pinkish-red residue from the Rayburn was left to cool in the garden, and was then thrown away, whereas the wood ash from the open fires, in the other rooms downstairs, was kept—to feed the roses. The Rayburn was our hearth; at one time this kind of stove, which served to heat the house and the water, to dry socks, to bake and cook and warm dishes, was the latest thing in domestic comfort and economy. To my mother it was a symbol of the grim, grinding foreignness of her new English country life: in the daytime when my father was at the office, it was she who went out into the cold with the scuttle to replenish the coal, for there never seemed enough to keep the fire glowing sufficiently to warm us or the house. But my father believed in the Rayburn: he gave me shares in the company for my twenty-first birthday.

If he had lived, my father would be ninety now; my mother left the chill and draughty house in the country after he died. But the Rayburn and the roses are still intertwined in my mind, and I gave Guinée to a friend when he moved to a cottage in Devon in the West Country under the lea of Dartmoor, and then as we grew closer, I went to stay with him from time to time, and then more and more often until we were living together. The cottage also has a Rayburn, and in the first weeks of our new love we triumphed over the strain of early hours struggling to keep it alight, of coal heaving and riddling and raking and dusting and floor mopping. I began to replant the garden, which had been much neglected, and he made arrangements to convert the stove to oil. One day a lorry appeared and installed a tank at the bottom of the garden; this will be screened by a trellis. The coal bunker has gone, the oil flows to feed the fire night and day, carefree. This summer, his Guinée, planted last year, flowered for the first time. I cut it and brought it into the study. The petals fell a day or two later on his desk: the scent still hangs about the shrivelled flowers, and the depth of the colour is a rich, sooty brown-black when they dry.

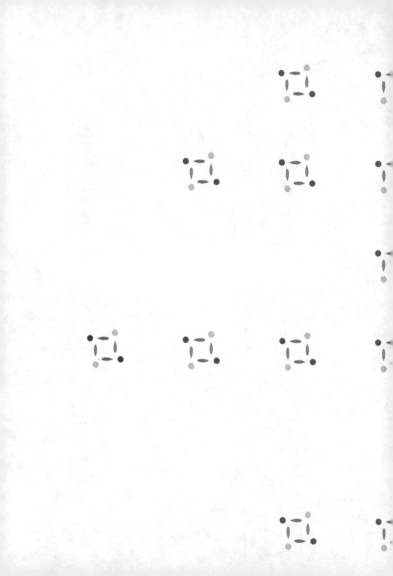

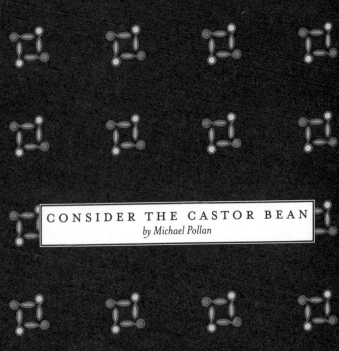

CONSIDER THE CASTOR BEAN
by Michael Pollan

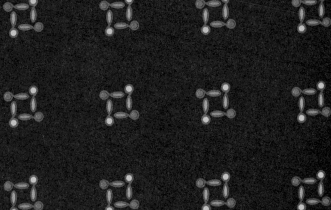

PRETTY THEY ARE NOT. BUT A GARDEN can labor under a surfeit of prettiness, be too sweet or cheerful for its own good. Sometimes what's needed in the garden is a hint of vegetal menace, of nature run tropically, luxuriantly amuck. For this I recommend the castor bean.

I grow them each spring from seed, indoors or out (not that they *need* the leg up of an indoor start), and by the end of the season these peculiar annuals will attain startling proportions: 12 feet in a good year for the green-leafed variety, slightly less for the (otherwise superior) red. I swear you can see this plant grow, all but hear the creak of its segmented, rhubarby stalk as its cells heroically stretch and divide. Each spring I'll give a spare seedling to an unsuspecting friend or two and can reliably expect an alarmed phone call by August demanding to know what the hell is this *thing* that is disturbing the peace of their property. No one can fail to notice a castor bean plant or form an opinion of it; like the party guest with the outsize personality, it can single-handedly alter the weather in a room. I should add that all the people to whom I've introduced the plant have invited it back, begging me the following spring for a transplant or seed.

Only a sunflower seed can perform a comparable prodigy in a summer, and in my garden the two giants vie for airspace and attention, though they could scarcely be more different in temperament or effect. Indeed, I've come to think of the castor bean as the slightly evil twin of the sunflower, beginning with the seed of the castor bean itself—a fat mottled bean that resembles (and in Latin—*Ricinus*—is named for) an engorged dog tick. Far from being tasty and nourishing like the sunflower's seed, the castor bean's is poisonous: three of them can kill a man.

But even if you didn't know this, you would know from its appearance that the castor bean is the gothic double of the sunflower, its Mr. Hyde. While the latter's cheery disk follows the sun across the sky like a happyface, the castor bean refuses to ingratiate itself, keeping its strange, spiky flower close to the vest, down below the eight-fingered hands of its dark, leathery leaves. And where the sunflower's flower is as clear as day, all its parts—petal, stamen, stigma, etc.—exposed, familiar, and intelligible, the castor bean's sexual organ is an alien, asymmetrical contraption of the sort a Dr. Seuss might conceive. Instead of petals it has a half-dozen prickly marbles airbrushed in a Day-Glo pink. These off-putting little fruits crown a turgid stalk from which, lower down, juts an off-kilter array of tiny whitish protuberances that look very much like miniature cauliflowers. The flower gives the impression of slightly kinky plant sex, though the precise mechanics of the act aren't at all obvious. It turns out that the female part is the spiny pink thing (each of which will manufacture a single bean), with the miniature cauliflowers holding out the male bits; bees effect the necessary commerce, though with no discernible enthusiasm. There's something cartoonishly sinister about the castor bean's flower. I'm not sure whether it's the inflamed hue or the angry prickles, which look sharp enough to draw blood. In actuality, they are as soft as whiskers (the Dad kind), though the chances that you'd actually venture a finger to find that out are slim to nil. I'm afraid this is one flower only a Morticia Addams could love.

I probably haven't sold too many castor beans yet—and it's a good thing this is not a seed catalogue. I haven't even gotten to the subject of castor oil—an unhappy association a great many people still bring to the castor bean plant. Mussolini used to torture his political prisoners by forcing them to imbibe huge quantities of castor oil, which is pressed from the bean after the deadly shell has been removed. But how many American children are still tormented by castor oil? Though it remains on the laxative shelf at the drugstore, my parents' generation was probably the last to gag at the sight of a spoonful; presumably there soon won't be many gardeners left who hold such a memory against the plant.

Let's hope so, because the plant has much to recommend it besides its unmatched scale. The glory of the castor bean (at last!) is its leaf, which is one of nature's most extravagant: large as a pie (one of them could give shade to a head of the largest size), and deeply divided into an eight-rayed star that is held aloft on its thick stem like an upturned palm. Emergent leaves wear a fine sheen that dries to a dark matte green or, in the case of the redder ones, to a warm carmine that's vividly set off by the veins, which run bright, bright red. For some reason *Ricinus* leaves are always perfectly formed and, even into September, when most leaves bear the wounds and blemishes of a long summer's struggle, they remain fresh as spring. Could it be their toxicity keeps pests from marring their perfection? Whatever the reason, the leaf and in turn the plant has a surprisingly kempt appearance for such a big fellow.

A single castor bean plant makes such a strong impression in the garden, is so *sui generis* (at least in the northern latitudes), that for a long time I was unsure exactly how to use it—exotic specimens, castor beans didn't seem to *go* with anything. I usually planted a few in and around the vegetable garden to divert attention from the late summer chaos, letting them mingle in the high society of cornstalks, sunflowers, and runner beans. That worked well enough, and had the added advantage of discouraging the moles, who are apparently as sickened as we are by the secretions of this plant. One gardening authority (Josephine Neuss, in *The Country Garden*) advises owners of new houses marooned on bare lots to plant rows of castor beans for a quick hedge or screen, but only until they can afford proper shrubbery. "Like junk jewelry they are not going to fool anyone," she cautions, "but they will decorate your property in an incredibly short time." Though one of the few writers to give more than a passing mention to the castor bean, Neuss isn't at all sure how she feels about the plant. She allows that though "they are certainly striking . . . these tropical giants would look ridiculous near a country farm house or any traditional form of fine architecture—unless your sense of humor is even more distorted than mine."

Well, perhaps mine is, because I've lately found other uses for *Ricinus*. A tall wall of dark green castor leaves makes a striking backdrop for a cutting garden, underscoring the tropical extravagance of my annuals while taking nothing away from their show. This season I plunked a few red castor beans in the back of a new border that had a few holes in it and was surprised to discover how well they can get along in a mixed border; provided, that is, your taste runs to the larger and less subtle plants—to the taller eryngiums and plume poppies, the Rastafarian nicotianas and the rougher roadside mulleins. Especially in midsummer, before the castor beans have begun to tower unreasonably, their warm-toned leaves look darkly handsome in the company of plume poppies and Scotch thistles—cool blue characters with leaves of a comparable magnitude and bizarreness.

It is often said that flowers count for less and less the longer one gardens, yet the border built around its foliage can't work in the absence of powerful contrasts, not just leaf against leaf, but garden against landscape. Especially here in New England, where, by midsummer, my hillside garden is up against such an onslaught of native green that it would disappear altogether if not for the unmistakable presence of the castor bean and its ilk—the defiantly non-native and monstrous, the formidably weird and ungreen, the horticulturally gothic.

Sometimes prettiness doesn't quite cut it. I suspect it was partly for this reason that the great eighteenth-century landscape designers always made sure to include a note of mortality in their compositions—a gothic ruin, a forbidding grotto, a scary chunk of statuary. They wanted the passing cloud of some *memento mori* to briefly darken the sweet pastoral scene, inducing a tinge of melancholy in the visitor and, perhaps, rendering the pretty more poignant. William Kent went so far as to plant dead trees in his gardens on the theory that if a garden was to be a world unto itself, it had better make room for the darker shades of feeling as well as the sunny ones. It's easy to make fun of this, yet I often wonder if our less-tortured gardening hasn't grown too wholesome and cheerful for its own good. So I make room for a few of these darkly gorgeous, otherworldly plants and invite them in to haunt my garden. My sunflowers have never looked more heartbreakingly sunny.

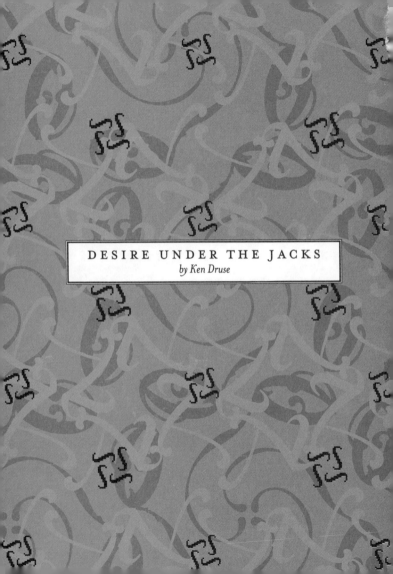

DESIRE UNDER THE JACKS
by Ken Druse

I DO NOT RECALL THE FIRST FLOWER name I ever spoke—probably "daisy." But one childhood memory of a plant is vivid. It was spring, over four decades ago. While walking with my mother in the woods near our home in New Jersey, I encountered a curious creature. My mother introduced the plant and whispered, "Jack-in-the-pulpit," words I'm sure I didn't understand. Then she delicately lifted the flower's flared cowl to reveal a tiny man playing peek-a-boo. It was a predictable intrigue for a kid, a confidence shared in hushed tones: here was a concealed holy man poised to baptize the uninitiated.

The flower or, rather, the flowering apparatus of *Arisaema triphyllum* is typical of the genus, having a slender spadix (Jack) inside a hooded spathe (pulpit). Jack's spadix sports tiny stemless flowers, and his spathe is decorated with stripes of light and dark green, or even cream and aubergine. This hood gives rise to another common name, cobra lily.

The first sign of growth from the *Arisaemas* is a stiff pole pushing one to two feet up through the soil like a charmed reptile. The shaft is wrapped in a leopard-spotted sheath camouflaged in woodland colors. *A. triphyllum* is one of North America's two native forest species; the other, *A. dracontium*, is the rare green dragon. The jack-in-the-pulpit has one or two trilobed leaves arranged in a T, whereas the green dragon's compound leaves may be divided into seven to fifteen segments on 30-inch-tall plants. The serpentine allusion is obvious when you see the plant's coiled 6-inch-long spadix extension darting out from the green spathe.

Many species produce a jutting "tongue" from their spadices, and some produce outgrowths from the spathe tips, which prompt their vernacular classification as "whiplash" *Arisaemas*. An extraordinary example is the prized *Arisaema griffithii*. Its chocolate-brown spathe is etched with parallel lines down its mid-rib and a tracery of yellow-ocher netting over puckered lobes. The spadix of *A. griffithii* casts out a 30-inch-long line. This appendage could be for show. But it more likely serves as a causeway to conduct crawling insect pollinators to this cobra lily's awaiting flowers.

However, there are more conventionally handsome species to tempt even the faint of heart. The comely *Arisaema candidissimum* from China has a 4-inch-tall pretty pink-and-white spathe that candidly flashes its translucent spadix. The Japanese species, *Arisaema sikokianum*, produces two leaves that vary by individual, from ones that are solid green to others with bright silver zones. Its richly striped spathe frames a brilliant white spadix shaped like an upended porcelain pestle.

I imagine these days that the easily cultivated *A. sikokianum* might provoke a weary "been there, done that" from jaded collectors. But species like the uncommon *A. candidissimum*, the bizarre *A. griffithii*, and even the familiar jack have not evolved putrid smells and colors reminiscent of carrion to titillate supernatural gardeners. These enticements have evolved for sex—to seduce pollinators into helping gametes mingle and make seed. Still, it is easy to arouse the gardener with this genus in the aroid family. *Arisaema ringens*, for instance, has large lustrous three-part leaves up to a foot across that form a bush concealing firm celadon spathes held like fists. The long-lasting floral stalks have green or black "lips" that curve along the spathe edges and flick at the base.

Sexual analogies are unavoidable, with labial lips and phallic spadices. A tropical *Arisaema* relative has the generic name of *Amorphophallus*—you know why. A European cousin, *Arum maculatum*, has several ribald common names, such as the "cuckoo pint," from the Anglo-Saxon words *cucu* for lively and *pintle* for penis. The plant's forceful thrust out of the ground from a dormant bulbous tuber sparked the charming moniker "Kitty-come-down-the-lane-jump-up-and-kiss-me." Could a child's early attraction to jack-in-the-pulpit be proof of psychosexual development? Is an unflagging attraction to the *Arisaema* a sign of sexual immaturity? If a jack-in-the-pulpit shows me its pintle, should I show it mine?

In the case of the jack-in-the-pulpit (or perhaps Jill), sexuality is enigmatic. Although many plants in nature bear only male or female flowers, several *Arisaema* species are endowed with the extraordinary ability to change sex. They may be boys or girls depending on the conditions of the previous growing season. In the case of *A. triphyllum*, the gender bending may take place annually over the course of its twenty-five-year life span. In lean times, the plant bears pollen as a male. In some years, there will be no flower spike at all. But pumped up after a season of ample rainfall, good light, and favorable temperatures, *A. triphyllum* may grow to 2 feet and become a fruiting female.

I have about one hundred *A. triphyllum* grown from the seeds of plants that I discovered on my property. I collect the berry-covered "cobs" in autumn, soak the fruits overnight in water, and then squeeze out the seeds. After washing them clean of any pulp, I roll the seeds up in moist sphagnum moss and place the wad in a sandwich bag labeled with the name, origin, and date of the contents. The package goes into the refrigerator for an artificial eight-week winter, after which a dozen seeds are sown just below the surface of a well-drained humusy medium in a 4-inch pot. Next the pot goes to the basement to bask in the eerie violet glow of 40-watt fluorescent tubes.

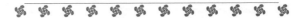

In two to four weeks, each seed produces a single blade. When the leaf becomes limp and turns the color of straw, I know little tubers have formed. I pop the pots back into the refrigerator for their second winter. After chilling, I plant the quarter-inch tubers in a permanent site outdoors. This time the leaves emerge like harpoons whose blades unfurl into a three-part leaf. These are very easy plants to germinate and grow, providing the seeds are fresh. Dried seed that I receive from fellow *Arisaema* freaks may take two years to sprout.

Many plantaholics have caught *Arisaema* fever, further enlarging the number of specialized horticultural groups. Rhododendron maniacs argue about the fairest darling, while others worship at the roots of the antique rose. Hostaphiles embrace their genus and never tire of debating how to nuke whichever garden critter favors their favorite. Unfortunately, the mounting zeal for the *Arisaemas* has led to a condition common among members of all specialty plant groups—plant one-upmanship: "My *Arisaema* is bigger than yours." If you cannot imagine a society devoted to a plant, think of an-

tique car collectors who narrow their focus to '57 Chevys (or the fanaticism of the Hummel cult). And if serious amateur and professional enthusiasts speaking in tongues seems strange, compare Latin names to the gigabyte-geek-speak of the computer literati.

I have stalked the wild jacks vicariously by visiting *Arisaema* Websites where zealous Internuts share their cliff-hanging tales of expeditions in Asia. There may be as many as 250 known *Arisaema* species and varieties worldwide. Species can be found in Tanzania and North America, but most come from southwest China, in Yunnan and Sichuan. Other *Arisaemas* originate in the Himalayas, Taiwan, Japan, and one grows as far north as the Russian island of Sakhalin. These days, collectors are also environmentalists and plants are not stolen from the wild. Most often, a few seeds are taken, though threatened plants are rescued from impending development. The ease of propagation may make all these species and cultivated varieties available to home gardeners through nurseries.

So far, I've limited my hunting to the pages of nursery catalogues, plant society seed exchanges, and local rescue missions. But my devotion is nonetheless heartfelt. Ever since I fell under the spell of these intriguing plants, I have wanted to raise as many different kinds as I can. The provocative shapes and unusual colors fascinate me as a plant enthusiast, and their swift emergence from tuber to flower satisfies me as a gardener. Some people who have become infatuated with the *Arisaema* clan may find the plants sinister and malevolent, mysterious or erotic. I think they are cute— weird but amiable. I love the *Arisaemas*, and my passion intensifies as I get older and learn more about them. If loving such a plant is a sign of arrested development, so be it. Sex, after all, like gardening is one of the few interests that last a lifetime.

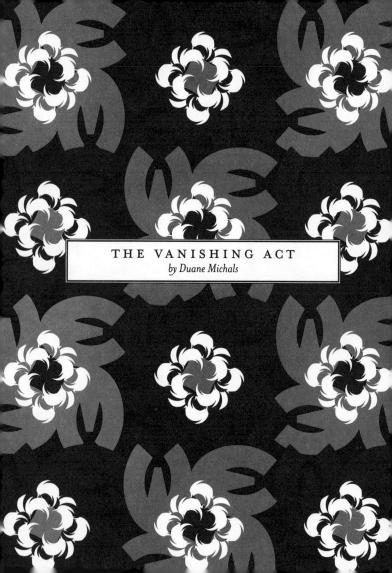

THE VANISHING ACT
by Duane Michals

WILLIAM BLAKE WOULD LIKE MY garden. It is a green mossy cabinet of floral curiosities where every ordinary bloom has a soul and is more bizarre than any black hole full of falling stars. Living people do not know that the glow of fireflies is the light of flower sprites' last good-byes before they die. Should children catch a firefly in a jar, that night will be dimmer by one star. With the first gleam of morning rays, the garden is a prism of a thousand hues refracted in tiny dots of crystal dew, a dazzling quilt of millefleur colors covering the sleeping flower beds. These bouquets seduce both butterflies and me with their siren scents and mesmerize my eyes with petal shapes that curve with the grace of adolescent thighs. Flowers construct the most charming geometries: circles like the sun, ovals, cones, curlicues and a variety of triangular eccentricities, which when viewed with the eye of a magnifying glass seem a Lilliputian frieze of psychedelic silhouettes.

Some blossoms twinkle in the gloaming's velvet shade and spiral flowers build their towers ever higher towards the ceiling of the sky to greet Icarus near the sun. Other creepers crawl like the tortoise, which left all alone soon toddles into every corner. Posies pulse with a slight vibration, a sensation more sensed than seen by poets and their kind. It is a sign that in this place, as in heaven, all things grow with grace and are in rhyme.

Most flowers have such lovely names, like hyacinth and Queen Anne's lace, though I do find spider wort and deadly nightshade sort of scary. Alas, some flowers also use an alias: witch hazel's nom de plume is *Hamamelis*; foxglove also known as *digitalis*. Even the common dandelion changed its appellation from *Dent-de-lion*, its Gallic derivation. Metaphysicians know that the sounds of words can reverberate with a subtle power. In ancient Druid days, in the bleakest winter hours, shaman priests would offer up an incantation of floral names, a mantra chant to lure the sun's return so life would warm and grow, as it still does today.

In this green menagerie there are colors only bees can see, too slight for human sight. Some tones, like blĭtz blau and quark bone, can only be observed by ladybugs in the dark. Then there's the color grim, which, much like soot and pĭtch, is blacker than de Sade's sins; also shimmering reds and that translucent faĭthful opaline. The florets of the nearby fickle plant change color like a chameleon when tickled by a tender zephyr's touch—first tangerine, then zebra strĭpes, now true salmon pink wĭth freckles of spotted blue. It seems as if a rainbow fell to earth here in a clump of colors each on top of one another.

Flowers are most natural in displaying their desires. But sorcerers warn us to be wary of the lovely lĭthium, that most cunning voluptuary. It arches ĭts stamen in the air, quivering wĭth lust, and should your hand be passing there, wĭth the slightest touch you will be kissed wĭth pollen dust. If the garden troll should see this telltale mark, in a jealous pique, he will cast a nasty spell and make you and your lover part.

When I take my midnight walk to see what secrets I can see, the garden slumbers in July's full moonlight, washed in a haze of lunar white as if there had been a summer's frost. I too look the color of chalk. The garden is a nighttime negative of its daylight self, and all is hushed but the cricket reveler's company. In the shadow of a shadow, an invisible cat catches a mouse and brings its trophy to the house. All seems quiet, calm, serene, with posies cast as players in my midsummer night's dream; poppy plays the part of Puck, a zinnia is the zany Bottom, and daisy was all wrong as Oberon. This should be the perfect moment for enlightenment, and that is why no light is seen, no sign is sent.

Sometimes on a summer's noon, clouds bloat with moisture like swelling black balloons and burst with rain and thunder tunes. At first, drops of water fall so slowly you could count them one by one. Suddenly, a Hiroshige print deluge—concentric circles crowd the mirror of the pond. Little pools form in the crotches of begonia's besotted leaves, and tree trunks shine like licorice sticks. Tiny fountains splash everywhere, off every leaf waterfalls drip, and little rivulets lick the budding stems. Fissures appear in the yellow sedum paths, impromptu streams with flotsam twigs spin past, and monk's hoods curtsey in raucous gusts of wind. Stoic robins sit in their jostled nests, while enduring nature's tantrum test. Even jack-in-his-pulpit isn't dry, and I stand under the cherry tree drenched in the silver rain, at last noticing that I am wet.

This monologue which you have read of my *jardin extraordinaire* has been but prologue to a secret which I now share. Of all the wonders in this wondrous domain, where I reign the gardener king, the flower I love most is the Lycoris, the mysterious Resurrection lily: that perfect symbol of the Christian myth. This bloom, in a feat more amazing than Houdini's gifts, sprouts in June such lush green foliage, then retreats and vanishes as if it had been just a memory in a forgotten dream. And where it was, nothing now is seen. Then all at once in late August's heat, tall leafless stalks crowned with iridescent pink and purple blossoms burst from their purgatory in the earth. This arcane act of nature, though perceived by us as ordinary, is a manifestation of Maya's phantom play, the great immensity expressed in every way. My garden is the universe. I am the universe. I am my garden. All things are the same.

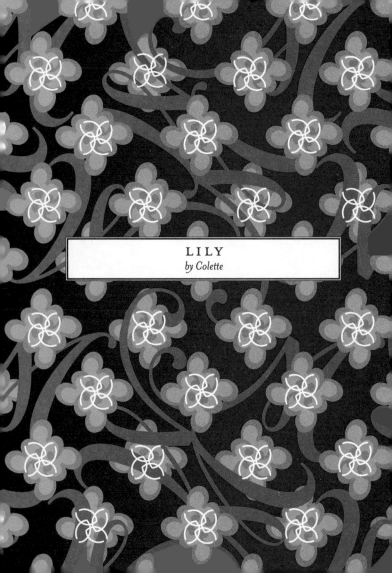

LILY
by Colette

Lys! et l'un de vous tous pour l'ingénuité.

WHAT I HAVE TO SAY ABOUT IT I say by way of ruse and rote. In the presence of a lily, or several lilies, a voice from the group is always raised to quote Mallarmé with literary fervor:

Lys! et l'un de vous tous pour l'ingénuité.

Since I am alone today, and since my daughter came and left me a lily, I did not fail to exclaim to myself, *"Lys! et l'un de vous tous . . ."* But my heart wasn't in it. Nor my intonation. I was embarrassed as I am when I try on a friend's feathered hat or her earrings and I see consternation written on the faces around me. I would like to give it another try, beginning a line higher to work up to it:

Droit et seul, sous un flot antique de lumière,
Lys! et l'un de vous tous pour l'ingénuité. *

---

* Lone and erect, beneath light's primal flood,
A lily! and pure as any one of you.
(*trans. by Richard Howard*)

But let's not dwell on this any longer. It requires greater art and greater love than mine—Henri Mondor, forgive me!—to do justice to a poem whose glory was assured by the music of Claude Debussy.

I date from far enough back for certain details from my antiquity to amuse me. When *L'Après-midi d'un faune* was surrounded on the one side by denunciation and on the other by spirited enthusiasm, I had already seen the passing of the time when Jules Lemaître—in the *Revue Bleue*, I believe—"explained" (*sic*) to the masses the little poem by Verlaine:

*L'espoir luit comme un brin de paille dans l'étable*** . . .

I have not forgotten that, on so unexpected a task of mediation, the future author of *La Massière* hazarded more wit than understanding, and more ridicule than wit. Did he bring the same hand, with

* Hope glimmers like wisps of straw in the shed . . .

the same heaviness, to bear on Mallarmé? Talk of it never reached me. Around the pagan triad I perceived only a buzzing of bees, the discreet scandal surrounding *L'Après-midi d'un faune*, when the commentators emphasized the fact that the sensual diversions of the cloven-hoofed faun and the two nymphs composed an uneven grouping.

I knew nothing of the poet as a man. His pleasant, distinguished face, with its goatee, has passed quite near me. I never saw Erik Satie, who dismissed one of my husbands with a wave of his hand. Never saw Maupassant, who felt honor-bound to plunge into the Marne after one of those dinners known as "Scrubbers' Bamboulas" and not die of congestion as a result. Never met the arrogant scaly remnants of Barbey d'Aurevilly . . . Yet for several years I had the leisure of being their contemporary, if not their friend, of being simply one who had seen them. I value no document as I do the memory of the human face, the lingering impression of its color, the incision of the pupil, the radiant wheel of the iris, the forehead covered or bare, the mouth and its successive deteriorations, a mouth unfit to recite its own poem; but it was from just such a mouth that I would like to have heard:

Lys! et l'un de vous tous . . .

This lily to which today I owe my modest divagation stands on the mantelpiece, its one foot in water. With a pair of embroidery scissors, the florist has removed its little hammers of yellow pollen, without which it stands there, clean, mutilated, and sad. Prior to it, all winter long, we could have had—for a price—the greenish lily, which blesses the union of so many young English brides and grooms. Perfidiously scented, the greenish lily can also speak and petition, imploring a disinclined virgin to love. I know nothing more about it, rarely associating with any but the white lily, which I call, wrongly, the true lily. This one here is white, fleshy, long-legged, and for floribundance fears none. It is a terrible pity that it is nearly always infested with Crioceris. The Crioceris is the red kiki, and the red kiki is the Crioceris. If you close a kiki up in your hand, it immediately makes a plaintive little cry with its wing sheath. The only time you call it Crioceris is when it fouls the lily with its dejecta, in the garden.

The true lily's favorite soil is the kitchen garden's, with tarragon, sorrel edgings, and purple garlic for neighbors. A patch of carrots, and a few nice rows of lettuce, yes, it likes that, too. In the garden of my childhood, its dazzling blooms and its fragrance were lords of the garden. While I was out hunting the red kiki, Sido, my mother, sitting inside the house, would call out to me, "Shut the garden door a little, those lilies are making the drawing room uninhabitable!"

And she would let me harvest them like hay and carry them in sheaves to Mary's altar when it was time for the May crowning. The church was stuffy and hot, and the children were laden with flowers. The unruly smell of the lilies would grow thick and interfere with the singing of the hymns. Several of the faithful would get up and rush out; some would let their heads droop and then fall asleep, overcome by a strange drowsiness. But the plaster Virgin, standing on the altar, would be brushing, with the tips of her dangling fingers, the long, half-open cayman jaws of a lily at her feet, smiling down at it indulgently.

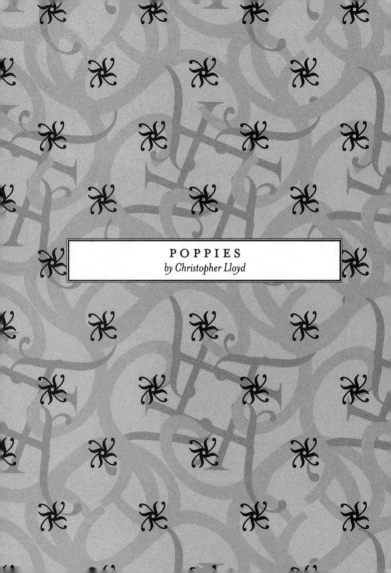

POPPIES
by Christopher Lloyd

POPPIES HAVE A PERSONAL MESSAGE for each of us; they are everyone's favourite. But why? And how?

First, there is the way they open. The bud is demure, yet suddenly, at sunrise, it bursts its stays. The two halves of the green, enclosing calyx are summarily discarded. For a while, and before they shrivel, they can hang around and their boat shape be admired. In fact, they can be floated in a bird-bath and given a few moments' attention before they are forgotten entirely.

Meantime, the flower's magic act is being rapidly performed. Its brilliantly coloured petals expand with visible impatience from their crumpled ball. How, one wonders, can all those creases possibly be ironed out? But it happens as you watch, as when a butterfly emerges from its chrysalis, dries and expands its wings. Poppies include every colour of the rainbow and every intermediate shade.

In the Oriental poppy, the centre is a dramatic focal point. The familiar poppy head is surrounded by a wealth of purple-black stamens. These stamens

❋ ❋ ❋ ❋ ❋ ❋ ❋ ❋ ❋ ❋ ❋ ❋

are like flowers themselves; they need to open in order to shed their pollen. If I am picking poppies for an arrangement, I like to be out before breakfast and I choose blooms in which the anthers have not yet broken open, knowing that these are the ones that will stay with me longest before fading.

When the anthers spill their pollen, the bees are ready. You see wild bumblebees, in particular, rolling about in ecstasy, tumbling with abandon, and picking the pollen up all over their furry bodies. By the time they are finished, the transformation from bud to bloom is complete.

When the petals fall, the poppy head takes over as a second attraction. A knob of increasing size, it seems that no one entering my garden, which is open to the public, can resist breaking it off. This, for me, is the downside of poppy growing. The complete poppy plant, with its handsome structure, is forcibly castrated as it runs to seed. All that remains after this violation is a naked stem, with nothing to crown it. Why do they do it? The seeds are still many weeks from being ripe. Is it ignorance that makes the violator think otherwise, or is it simply that if a knob presents itself, it is there to be snapped off?

But in your own, unshared garden (I enjoy sharing mine), your poppies will progress triumphantly to the final stage, when the seeds, which are small and abundantly produced, are ripe. A circle of pores opens, close to the ridged cap, which is the top of the capsule, and whenever the wind blows and shakes the pod, like a pepper pot, out blow some more seeds.

The Oriental poppy, *Papaver orientale*, has the largest blooms—larger than those of any other hardy perennial except its rival, the peony. And, in nature, they are scarlet—a brilliant, pure, unalloyed, unashamed, flaunting scarlet. What a wonderful, vibrant colour that is! Fit to make the pulse quicken in anyone with blood in their veins. I love the scarlet poppy, and we have more of it than of any other variety. But another that vies with it in my affections is the poppy called 'Goliath,' after the giant Philistine who struck terror in the hearts of the Israelites until David, whose mother had not stopped him from playing with a catapult as a child

※ ※ ※ ※ ※ ※ ※ ※ ※ ※ ※ ※

(as mine did me, because it is a dangerous toy), allegedly felled him with a stone. Well, I don't know about that. It was a long time ago and myths are apt to build up around heroes. All I can say is that my 'Goliath' poppies are tall and sturdy and do not get felled, although in fairness I will add that I garden on a singularly stone-free clay soil.

'Goliath' grows 4 feet tall and has the hugest blooms of any poppy. They are rich crimson, which is as exciting as scarlet. In choosing plant neighbours to vie with it, I have been best pleased with an equally bright and pure yellow giant buttercup, *Ranunculus acris* 'Stevenii.' It is, however, shocking to discover that there are some gardeners (and non-gardeners) of a congenitally weak and palsied constitution who do not like strong colours and who even pride themselves, as a class apart, on their good taste. The good-taste brigade can only think comfortably in terms of colour harmonies and of soft and soothing pastel shades.

The market never misses an opportunity, and many named varieties of Oriental poppy have been developed in colours that are acceptable in the

❄ ❄ ❄ ❄ ❄ ❄ ❄ ❄ ❄ ❄ ❄ ❄ ❄

politest circles. (I grow some of them myself.) 'Perry's White' was one of the earliest; clearly a plant in need of a visit to the laundry, its indeterminate colouring merges at the centre of the flower into an indeterminate, darker blotch. 'Black and White' is bolder and more distinct, with a big, black, basal blotch. 'Cedric's Pink' is quiet and coy. 'Juliane' is quite a flashy girl, in her way, with frilly, overlapping petals on a large, salmon-pink bloom. 'Beauty Queen' is, I would say, ill served by its name, but is a soft, luminous shade of orange.

I took a fancy to 'Beauty Queen' in a friend's garden in Scotland in June, when it was flowering, and received permission to take a piece. When you see a plant that you must have, the answer to the question "Would you like some at the right time?" should be "I'd rather have it now," right time or not. Otherwise, the right time will surely slip by, the transference of the coveted piece from central Scotland to the south of England (or from California to Maine) will be inconvenient, and all you'll have is a gnawing gap in the pit of your wish-world.

I scrabbled around the side of 'Beauty Queen'

until I found one or two of its fleshy roots and took them home with me in a plastic bag. Cut into 4-inch lengths, they were potted upright in a light compost and went into a cold frame, providing me in due course with three nice plants.

The most general propagation method for Oriental poppies is from root cuttings, and the time of year when you make them seems not greatly to matter. Plants with fleshy roots intensely dislike being moved, however, and generally sulk awhile. But in transferring them, the chances are that you will leave behind the broken roots and that they will make new plants on the old site.

Many of the most delightful poppies are annuals. It is a thrilling sight in early summer to see a neglected cornfield, in which herbicides have not been used, ablaze with wild scarlet poppies, probably *Papaver rhoeas*. Roadside verges, where the soil has been disturbed by recent roadworks, are another area where poppy seeds that have remained dormant for decades, waiting their opportunity, suddenly find it there, and cause unlooked-for traffic problems as motorists suddenly brake in order to

❋ ❋ ❋ ❋ ❋ ❋ ❋ ❋ ❋ ❋ ❋ ❋

have a better look. (Gardeners and naturalists must be the most dangerous class of drivers; something the insurers have yet to notice.)

These field poppies need disturbed soil, free of competing grasses and other perennials, in order to flourish. Remember that, if you want them in your own garden. Don't try to grow them in ground that you want to leave undisturbed.

Plant breeders have done a great deal of work on the field poppy and have often succeeded in eliminating the scarlet element altogether, substituting it with—you've guessed it—cool greys, off-whites, and grubby mauves. However, any poppy lover should grow the new strain called Angel's Choir (oh dear!), developed by the seed firm Thompson & Morgan. It aims at double flowers in a great and beautiful colour range, including not only the soft shades but crimson, bright pink, and purple. The results are entrancing. You may sow directly where the plants are to flower, or you may sow a seed or two in each of a number of cells, treating the seedlings individually until they are planted out. This controlled method gives the

※ ※ ※ ※ ※ ※ ※ ※ ※ ※ ※ ※

finest results. The controlled method also works for another favourite annual poppy of mine, *Papaver commutatum*, often simply referred to as 'Lady Bird.' It is deep red, with a large black blotch at the base of each petal.

Of course, there are many other poppies. Some gardeners devote themselves to the genus *Meconopsis*, which includes the famous blue poppies, but to grow these without tears of frustration, you need to be assured of cool summers.

My final words shall be for the annual opium poppy, *Papaver somniferum*, which seed catalogues sedulously give any name other than the correct one. It makes a lovely plant, with smooth, grey, frilly-margined leaves that catch and hold the rain or dew, taking hours to dry out. There are many selected strains in a range of shades from white to black, though mauve is natural to this species. The fully double kinds will continue to remain true from self-sown seed for may years: *P. somniferum* is a great self-sower. You may call it a weed, and you may have to pull out 99 of its 100 seedlings, but no one could be cross with this poppy for very long.

BUDS
by Karel Čapek

TODAY, ON THE 30TH OF MARCH, at ten o'clock in the morning, the first tiny blossom of forsythia opened. For three days I have been watching its largest bud, a tiny golden pod, so as not to miss this historic moment; it happened while I was looking at the sky to see whether it would rain. Tomorrow the twigs of forsythia will be sprinkled all over with golden stars. You simply cannot hold it back. Of course, most of all the lilacs have hurried up; before you notice it, they have made fragile and slender little leaves; you can never watch a lilac. *Ribes aureum* also opens its ribbed and pleated frills; but the other bushes and trees are still waiting for some imperative "Now!" which will breathe from the earth or from the sky; in that moment all buds will open, and it will be here.

Germination belongs to the phenomena which men call a natural process; it is, however, a real march. Decay is also a natural process, but it does not remind one of a march; I should not like to compose a *tempo di marcia* for the process of decay. But if I were a musician I should compose a "march

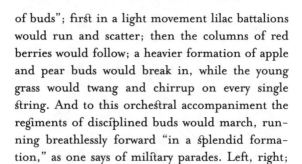

of buds"; first in a light movement lilac battalions would run and scatter; then the columns of red berries would follow; a heavier formation of apple and pear buds would break in, while the young grass would twang and chirrup on every single string. And to this orchestral accompaniment the regiments of disciplined buds would march, running breathlessly forward "in a splendid formation," as one says of military parades. Left, right; left, right: heavens, what a march!

One says that in spring Nature turns green: it is not quite true, for it also becomes red with pink and crimson buds. There are buds deep scarlet and rosy with cold; others are brown and sticky like resin; others are whitish like the felt on the belly of a rabbit; they are also violet, or blond, or dark like old leather. Out of some, pointed lace protrudes; others are like fingers or tongues, and others again like warts. Some swell like flesh, overgrown with down, and plump like puppies; others are laced into a tough and lean prong; others open with puffed and fragile little plumes. I tell you, buds are as strange and varied as leaves and flowers. There

will be no end to your discoveries. But you must
choose a small piece of earth. If I ran as far as
Benešov,* I should see less of the spring than if I sat
in my little garden. You must stand still; and then
you will see open lips and furtive glances, tender
fingers, and raised arms, the fragility of a baby, and
the rebellious outburst of the will to live; and then
you will hear the infinite march of buds faintly
roaring.

So! While I was writing this, the mysterious
"Now!" must have come: the buds which in the
morning were still swaddled in tough bands have
put forth fragile tips, sprigs of forsythia have begun
to shine with golden stars, the swollen pear buds
have unrolled a little, and on the points of some
other buds gold-green eyes are sparkling. Out of
resinous scales young green leaves are shooting, fat
buds have burst, and a filigree of ribs and folds
is emerging. Don't be shy, blushing little leaf;
open, folded little fan; awake, downy sleeper, the
order to start has already been given. Strike up

* A town about thirty miles from Prague.

fanfares of the unwritten march! Glisten and roll, pipe and sing, you golden brass, drums, flutes, and innumerable violins; for the silent brown and green little garden has set out on its victorious march.

HELLEBORE
by Colette

WHERE WE LIVE, AND TO A LESSER extent everywhere else, it is called the Christmas rose. Yet it does not resemble a rose, not even the little eglantine, nervous and blushing, except that it does have five petals like all the others.

A pebble, a blade of grass, a fallen leaf, all have more of a smell than it does. To be fragrant is not its mission. But let December come, let the wintry frost blanket us, and the hellebore will show you its true colors. A nice deep snow, not too powdery, a little heavy, and winter nights that the west wind passes through like a precursor, now that's what makes the hellebore happy. To the garden of my childhood, it was at the end of December that I would go, certain to find it there, and lift the slabs of snow that covered the winter rose.

Promised, unexpected, precious, and prostrate but fully alive, the hellebores hibernate. As long as they are weighed down with snow, they remain closed, ovoid, and on the outside of each furled convex petal a vaguely pink streak seems to be the only indication that they are breathing. The hardy,

star-shaped leaves, the firmness of the stems, so many characteristics through which the whole plant proclaims its touching, evergreen determination. When picked, its sensitive little shells undo their seams in the warmth of a room, unleashing the little tuft of yellow stamens, happy to be alive and spreading, free . . . Hellebore! When you are put into the hands of the florist, his first concern is to manhandle your petals, bending them back flat, just as he attempts to do to the tulip, torturing it to death. Behind his back, I undo his work of breaking and entering, and if I can promise you, in my house, water up to the neck and light up to the eyelashes, you can sleep out the remainder of your chaste slumber, then perish by the decision of human hands, when the warm snow might still have kept you alive, hellebore.

HELLEBORES
by Daniel Hinkley

I T HAS BEEN LONGER THAN A DECADE
now since I have come to know the hellebore. I
have sown its seed, grown resultant seedlings,
and waited for the inaugural blossoming. By
no means have I become an expert in ten seasons,
but I have had sufficient time to embrace this
genus, to learn of its subtleties and mysteries, its
demands and crankiness; certainly time enough to
conjure associations of hellebore season.

Hellebore season. It resonates with images and
aromas, so much like other short, yearly appoint-
ments with things we love; Walla Walla sweets,
Copper River reds, morel mushrooms. The time of
hellebores, though, is profoundly less carnal, with
its chilled, lean mornings and whisperings of
lengthening days. There may be at times the soft
rain that we welcome during the shy months, or
light snow, and perhaps the faintest trill of chick-
adees and bush tits. There is nothing so complex as
the garden of early summer, with nervous nesting
birds, maddening weeds, and wild colors that flash
and then evaporate.

Because of hellebores, my garden no longer

opens and closes like a book of seasons, or floods from blackness to brilliance at some mythical switch of light. The garden now simply narrows to that corridor of late summer, and moves on to late autumn, to the thin days of early winter, and then swells again in early spring. Certainly, it is not just the hellebore that takes me full circle. There are witch hazels and viburnums, the brilliant striated bark of maples and the precious flowers and foliage of cyclamen. In fact, dozens of plants beg me to stay the course; to wake and walk the garden in this quiet and cold season when most gardeners have retreated to the warm indoors. But in the midst of high summer's sultry, exuberant activity, it is the hellebores I look forward to most. With each turn of autumn leaf, and every morning frost that perches upon the garden, excitement mounts for what lies ahead, and I hold vigil for the first hellebore blossoms.

Hellebores are slow. Achingly slow to build in girth, and exasperatingly slow to push forth bud and blossom. In late autumn, if I dig with my fingers through the crowns of the plants, I can find the plump flower buds prepared for emergence. There is no pleading with them, no hoping for expedience. They tease with the same wrapped anticipation of a child's gift. And I know that, in this slow coldness, what takes so annoyingly long to begin will take an equally long period to complete. Hellebores have taught me the torment of slow motion in the garden, but also its astounding glory.

Then, the flowers: rarefied but brawny. Fluid, pale hues gradually intensify to supersaturated damsons, crimsons, and jades; butterscotch or pure white stars pierced with a boss of golden stamens. Nodding, shimmering satin cups that must be lifted for a full appreciation of the speckled inside, if speckling exists at all. None the matter. Look at this, the one we have called Mandela. Now, from mid-February to late May, the deepest, blackest blossoms are finally upon us. I round the corner, week after week, and come upon the nightfall blossoms facing the low-angled sun. Moments later, I turn my head for another glimpse, over my shoulder toward the morning light. The flowers are no longer the black of satin but that of the richest

Merlot held to a candle. Hellebores change by the moment and by the season; yet theirs is a methodical progression. Nothing here and gone. They age at the same pace as keg Scotch whiskey or a rich Gouda.

We porter pollen from flower to flower during this season: from a good grape to our best clear primrose; from a perfect pink goblet to a black picoteed with rose. With a simple brush to the stigma of the mother plant, we effect the release of dreams weighted with chromosomes, dreams carried down the style to the unfertilized ovules, dreams birthed by fertilization. When frigid air from the Gulf of Alaska glides southward and settles over our garden, the eager, open flowers deflate like punctured egos. Surely this time they cannot withstand this cold. Too far along in blossom, I think. Too cold. They lie defeated and water-soaked, an unshaven look of frost upon their tissue. On the third day, the winter storms move eastward and the grip of the cold weakens. In early morning, by the time I have risen to assess the damage, the hellebores are revived, but with the slightest sleepy yawn to their flowers. And then, like wings of butterflies that emerge damp and shriveled from a cocoon, they fully expand again.

We harvest our hopes in June, when they are black and shiny and they are quickly sown. In winter, the first of the seedlings appear. Leaf by leaf, the expectations grow, and then, the first blossoms in just a year. Some are better than others; some are disappointing and are released, and some gather us around like Druids to marvel. We have grown dreams for an entire year; large flowers of butter yellow, facing outward, of black purple like overripe grapes, or of flaring reds lit by the winter sun in this deeply quiet and slow garden.

Finally, the last flower fades to an almost imperceptible shade. The season has been long and we are full and satiated. Yet, though their leaves and stems are battered, and we are suffering the demands of a petulant summer garden, they are not ignored. In this flickering, swimming, drunken season of high gardening, I would not risk compromising their chances of storing the sun for the incoming winter. The winter ahead; the season of hellebores.

IRISES
by Katharine S. White

IF I AM LUKEWARM ABOUT THE DAHLIA, I am red hot about the bearded iris. I like it without qualification, and would not be without it in the garden. I happen not to care for the pink varieties that have become so popular lately, especially the horrid flamingo pinks, and prefer the whites, blues, violets, purples, yellows, and coppers, not only because they seem more like the flower in its natural state but also because they add such strong notes of color to the spring borders. I am not at all averse, though, to the ever-changing combinations produced by the hybridists. In fact, the infinite variations of color in the falls, the standards, and the beards of the new varieties are a part of their charm. Almost every color-illustrated iris catalogue that specializes in the new hybrids is a handsome one, since the bearded iris is the most photogenic of flowers. I shall mention only one, which is perhaps my favorite this year—that of Cooley's Gardens, in Silverton, Oregon. The gleaming illustrations show not only solo portraits of the beauties but also iris growing in masses or in groups in gardens and arranged in bowls. The iris hybridists whose originations Cooley's Gardens introduces are Hall, Kleinsorge, Gibson, and Riddle. One rhizome of one of their new varieties may cost as much as $25, but such high-priced ones are not a bit more beautiful than the ones that, because they are old favorites and in less short supply, cost only a dollar or two. The new Silvertone, at $20, a silvery pale blue with a tangerine beard, is exquisite, but so is Temple Bells, an apricot yellow with a heavy orange-red beard, at $2. If I were to choose one deluxe Cooley iris, it might be Frost and Flame, a Hall hybrid that is pure white with a tangerine beard, priced at $12—a delicious flower. And if you are searching for unusual iris, don't forget the Lamb catalogue, which even offers *twice-flowering* iris, that bloom both spring and fall. Except fragrance, that second blooming is the only thing the modern iris up till now has lacked—in my book, anyway.

BEARDED IRISES & PEONIES
by Henri Cole

BEARDED IRISES

I was a stranger and you welcomed me.
I thought: he will not stand for the stench
    of my body.
But truth is a bright needle pulling an ugly thread
and he opened his arms to take me in.
I thought: I love this ordinary man who is made
of the best intentions.
I thought: here's a man who will keep his promise.
In the bars, I was a doomed and lovely thing,
like a flower doomed by frost,
but now I have been redeemed.
I was thirsty and you gave me your glass.
I thought: he will be disgusted seeing wine
run into my open mouth, making my teeth shiver.
But it was dusk and the somber blue sky
began melting like an iris,
abstracting him into its fading light.
I was hungry and you gave me meat.
Eating vigorously with my hands,
I thought: I am like a bearded iris,
my ego unsubjugated.

I demand and get a bed of my own,
from which the whole world of the Not-Me
seems fatal and ridiculous.
I was naked and you clothed me.
I thought: he'll not let me wear his handsome
    red coat.
To different men come different blessings.
This was a coat worthy of Cocteau.
But you made me put it on.
I thought: now I am like a red boat,
blazing on a lake.
I was sick and you comforted me.
How I awaited your visits, as a caged dog
    awaits liberation,
your face—sculpted with little crow's-feet,
the mark of a man with an interior life—
healing me like the sun.
If I were in prison you would defend me.
I would think: one day soon I'll be home again.
I would think: how precious silver is
stolen from a man with a great estate,
a man I hate!

And when I die, you will bury me,
easing my corpse into the sepulcher,
as a rotting iris is plunged into compost.
A bare bulb at the center of the vault
will illuminate your face,
and I will think: nothing that comes after
could be as good as what came before.

PEONIES

Ample creamy heads beaten down vulgarly,
as if by some deeply sadomasochistic impulse,
like the desire to subdue, which is normal
    and active,
and the desire for suffering, which is not;
papery white featherings stapled to long stalks,
sopped with rain and thrown about violently,
as Paul was from his horse by the voice of Christ,
as those he judged & condemned were, leaving
    the earth;
and, deeper in, tight little buds that seem to blush
from the pleasure they take in being submissive,
because absolute humility in the face of cruelty
is the Passive's way of becoming himself;
the groan of it all, like a penetrated body—
those of us who hear it know the feeling.

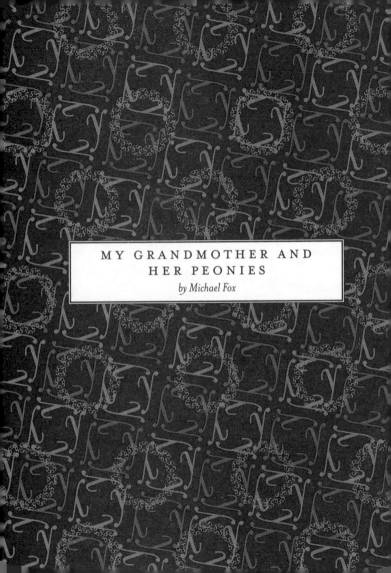

MY GRANDMOTHER AND
HER PEONIES

by Michael Fox

MY MATERNAL GRANDMOTHER'S garden outside New York contained Festiva Maxima peonies (*Paeonia lacti-flora* 'Festiva Maxima'), flowers I called "pom-poms" as a child. I was three or four years old, led by the hand between garden beds, out of which reached blooms the size of my head. I could see at eye level into the white depths of their petals, where bees buzzed and crawled—a lush, more vivid heaven than any pictured in Episcopal Sunday school. Now when I bend to a peony bloom its scent recalls this past, the elegant garden, its layout and borders. I want to recall also the exact feel of Gran's hand holding mine, the tall presence of her beside me in her pressed slacks and low-heeled slippers, but these sensations have to be mostly imagined; they are as hard to recall as the exact scent of a peony itself. When she was eighty-four and dying of colon cancer, Gran took her exit early, "taking her exit" being her euphemism, conceding to illness the inevitable but at her own pace. She had a supple hand on the reins, as she might have said, to the end.

She left behind an opulent house: deep enfolding chairs and couches, fine hand-painted screens, wonderful art; the cool fragrant rooms in which she had lived with these things. But of the opulence left behind when she was gone, her peonies were not least. My mother dug up the "eyes" of these the autumn my grandmother's house was sold. She replanted them in her own Vermont yard where there was still no garden, only a pond and an expanse of lawn. When the peonies broke ground the following spring their fine red stalks unfurled to green, and from the buds opened flowers as glorious as in memory. In that resurrection, obviously, what had been transplanted from Westchester to Vermont was mostly spirit.

One of Gran's candid sentiments was to say about a woman friend that growing up she'd had no home, and was for that reason a "kennel dog." I understood her to mean by this two things, both in sympathy: the creature that was not accustomed to the home, unacclimated to the parlor, unknowing how to behave. From this I inferred "kennel dog" might mean also the wandering soul that had no calm of place, shunting here and there all its life as though pursued.

A shrub or perennial bought from a nursery is like a kennel dog to me. It is in a category different from that of the cutting, seedling, or mature plant acquired from another garden or gardener. A nursery plant comes from parent stock in the same way as the slip or division I've acquired from a friend or neighbor, with only this difference: it has spent its life in a plastic pot, moving here and there on a truck bed, living on Peters and Pro-gro. I tell myself it is imaginative to think this makes any difference—then put the latest purchase out on the porch to harden off, acclimate, "learn how to be-have." I pity and want to console nursery plants for their hothouse tenderness, their lack of heritage, their lack of *ground*.

Gran's peonies stand at the other extreme of this bizarre discrimination, since the ground they come from is my own past. Their transference out of the past into the present is legacy, and it carries a light burden: the sole living remnant of a lost landscape will dictate the nature of its new surroundings. I'll say it was in their honor that my mother and I began to work in her yard—it's only a guess. But soon we were making walls of stone and laying out beds, apparently trying to make a garden as elegant as the one the peonies had come from.

It can't be broadly true, but every male gardener I know attributes the genesis of his interest in gardening to a grandparent. In their retirement from moneymaking and in their quieter, more nurturing attentions, grandparents might be well suited to unveiling this, the happy work of horticulture. In my own case, going through the vegetable garden with Gran was an easy pleasure uncomplicated by labor. The garden was situated on a broad natural terrace above the house; in June we cut flowers there, and in July we collected peas. On hot days in August we ate warm tomatoes off the vine.

Down in the house there was a staff and staff's quarters. There was "the man" to drive the car, "the girl" to wash the laundry and Mary Mack to cook the dinner. Outside the house, the lawns and gardens were tended by groundskeepers—we called them "the men." By vocation Gran was a sculptor, and in the working world she served many years on the board of Planned Parenthood. But the work of her home life was purely administrative: she had no other task but the management of staff. I remember she liked to give haircuts to her grandchildren, and to cut and arrange flowers: her diminished, overstaffed domestic life is illustrated to me in the memory of her doing these things—the movements of her hands, her delight—as though nothing in her life was as simple and pleasurable. Her hands moved similarly over the pieces of stone or clay she worked into sculpture, a lingering tender care that is vivid to my memory. It was as though these few manual tasks had been sanctified, raised or compressed to poetry, by the removal of any and all labor from her life.

This may have been just as she wanted it—or not.

She was more complicated than I can convey here. She had a decorative mania for all things *faux*.

I have from her house a fruit basket made all of wax, which sits under its own glass dome, and stone fruit—marble apples and pears of a really pleasing verisimilitude—on two-tiered porcelain salvers. My mother has *faux* vases piled with *faux* fruit and flowers made of painted tin. Which is to say that for all the do-lessness and perhaps isolation that her wealth caused her, Gran still thought money was pretty fun. In the attic she kept a huge trunk full of elaborate costumes for capers and plays that were the occasion for large parties, parties that were the occasion for singing and dancing and speechifying. She liked gaiety, as she called it, and her own sparkling moments define this word for me.

I remember her explaining that the ants which crawled over the buds of peonies before they bloomed were necessary. Without their help the sticky bud would remain locked, would blacken and shrivel without unfolding, and maybe this describes just the way she felt about her own wealth and position: money as tool and liberator—or what might simply make for gaiety, the release of bloom, if well used. I suppose I'm replying with the view that those ants sometimes spread botrytis (aside from wilt, the peony's only serious disease), as horticultural manuals would have it. *I* say it might have been better for her to be less protected, to have lived outside the hothouse, but she wouldn't have agreed. And I admit my dour objections are beside the point. It might be the same to say that peonies would be better off with less, when they're so heavy in their bloom and weak in their legs that they collapse under the added weight of dew. She knew what she'd been given and remained grateful for the gift of it always.

Peonies—the herbaceous ones I'm talking about—require for good flowering thirty to sixty days of frost: they're fussy in other words not for warmth but for cold. This is contrary and endearing, the bloom of tropical appearance that asks for snow. I've spent some years on the ever-temperate West Coast, where winter does not bring this month of freezing nights and where I have tried to feel the absence of peonies well compensated by other plants. But I'm giving it up. Kennel dogs find a home range somehow, however arbitrarily: I return to the Northeast in part because I'll go without fuchsia and agapanthus and a hundred other species before I will the jump-up and drop-dead glory of herbaceous peonies.

The last time I saw Gran she was slumped in the middle of her enormous bed with the window curtains drawn, in her bathrobe and with her hair not yet brushed. Her swollen legs were splayed before her, her hands hung limp, and the sight of her forced me to recognize that I'd never before seen this. I'd never seen her sit but two ways: with back straight, her hands in her lap, perched at the edge of her seat, or reclining in her place at the end of the long couch, one knee crossed over the other. At these moments, sitting in these ways, she was always poised. Now I was allowed to see something else, another sort of moment, and she with her plans must have known this moment would be our last. Certainly she was too sick to make the usual presentation of herself, but I want to think she also intended to be seen "as is." I have a recurrent imaginative vision when I recall this last meeting: it is of Gran pulling aside a curtain with a smile. There's a depth of space beyond her, white and without movement, and there's nothing in that space to focus on—there's nothing much to the vision. She's only opening a divider to invite me in— an admission of frailty from a matriarch, unveiling the greater grandeur of acceptance and grace.

Her last words were to her daughters: "Oh girls, isn't it wonderful, it's working already." The doctor at her bedside who had administered the lethal dose put away his things. He had been spirited into the house just minutes before, after the home-care nurse, a good woman of problematic religious convictions, had been taken to the movies for the night.

"Oh girls, isn't it wonderful . . ." There's no real locus for enthusiasm like this: it is wide-eyed, infectious; it seems to take in all of the world, and time—the look forward and the look back. Such gusto must be the best thing to cultivate in life, whenever possible: the absurdly lush flower, big as a plate and up from nothing, here and gone; tower-

ing foliage that deflates with frost and blackens on the ground in graphic death, then jumps up again from a winter's sleep—improbable, plucky, resplendent and impermanent, spring after spring after spring.

HARDY GERANIUMS
by Thomas C. Cooper

AMONG AN ASTONISHING NUMBER OF good deeds, Carolus Linnaeus, the father of modern taxonomy, committed one minor blunder that has caused confusion in the conversation of flower gardeners for 200-odd years. Somewhere in the process of classifying 12,000 plants, Linnaeus bundled together pelargoniums—'Martha Washington' and her friends, which grace containers, hanging baskets, and city park bedding schemes the world around—and geraniums, that group of some 300 species of largely hardy perennials. In doing so, he condemned generations of gardeners to flounder in uncertainty about which plants they were discussing, the tender summer pot plants or the hardy border plants. (In fact, not all geraniums are hardy; some of the most splendid are native to tropical places such as Madeira.) The enduring use of "geranium" is, in the words of Hugh Johnson, the author of *Principles of Gardening*, "one of the rare cases in horticulture where democracy has successfully routed botany."

Despite this continuing confusion, geraniums

have persevered, even achieving minor cult status; and with good reason, for they are one of the quintessential garden plants, equally at home in the border, the woodland, or the rockery. Indeed, were it not for their unassuming good looks, sturdy constitutions, and cheerful demeanors, hardy geraniums would make wonderful collectors' plants—those rarities of great refinement that are difficult to acquire and propagate and tricky to grow. But in truth they are easy to grow and propagate, long-flowering, great minglers, and forgiving of insults from gardeners. Some geraniums will even plug along happily in dry shade, the antithesis of all that is good and desirable in gardening.

Geranium flowers come generally in shades of red, blue, or white—from the startling shades of *Geranium psilostemon*, a piercing magenta with a hypnotic black eye, to the elegant 'Johnson's Blue,' resplendent with 2-inch gentle lavender-blue flowers, to a wide variety of "albums"—all white and all appropriate for making little Sissinghursts. In between, there are doubles, many wonderful pinks and roses, as well as mixtures—one shade with veining of another shade, or perhaps overlaid with a silvery wash.

You need not lie on your stomach to see the flowers or wait three years for a single bloom that lasts part of one evening. Geraniums such as 'A. T. Johnson,' 'Wargrave Pink,' and a number of others, commence flowering in early summer at a young age and are apt to keep producing their saucer-shaped blooms regularly until the end of autumn. Most flowers are modest in size—roughly two to three inches across—but they have abundant delicacy and charm. As prized as the flowers, the foliage of geraniums adds a refined, graceful touch to the garden, from the first days of spring to the final shudderings of autumn. The leaves are generally rounded and either deeply lobed—as in the scalloped and felted leaves of *Geranium renardii*—or heavily cut—as in *Geranium clarkei*, an intricate design with spidery green fingers.

Being diverse and sexually active plants, geraniums have developed out of their 300 species an assortment of some 500 cultivated plants, such as *Geranium phaeum* 'Samobor,' with dusky maroon flowers and cut leaves ringed by a band of brown, or *Geranium wallichianum* 'Buxton's Variety,' a late-blooming trailer with winsome blue flowers that change character and color as the season progresses, bringing color and a soft touch to the hard edges of a rock garden in autumn. The genus breaks loosely into three groups—low-growing mat formers, mounding clumpers, and trailers that fling out their arms to embrace all about them. Many members of the genus have dual personalities, able, for example, to grow in such broad and dense clumps that they become ground covers.

My first geraniums were mounding plants for the front and middle of the border, where they knit together different plantings while adding bursts of color throughout the summer. The combination of elegantly cut, lobed leaves and clear pink flowers make the hybrid 'A. T. Johnson' indispensable in any border composition. It is the sort of plant you can introduce to your mother without worry, a perfect plant for the novice who is uncertain about which colors go together, unaware that plants need staking, and still learning the other rules that one acquires over time. Later on, when a gardener has more courage, this plant will still be around—a steady friend able to draw out the best in any other plant, no matter what its temperament or flower color.

As with most geraniums, the foliage of 'A. T. Johnson' appears in early spring, first as small rosettes of two or three leaves that seem so meager I often fear the winter killed off my plants. But tiny, fully formed new leaves keep appearing on the soil surface, expanding and rising into 18-inch hummocks at about the time the daffodils start to teeter. They form almost perfect domes, giving a sense of order to summer borders that have not yet hit their stride. I think a broad pot planted with one clump of 'A. T. Johnson' would make an outstanding early-summer floral display.

The flowers on 'A. T. Johnson' are a soft, clear pink with a silvery sheen. This gloss gives them a brilliance that reinforces their delicate silkiness. How the plant manages this overlay I don't know. I can't imagine a flower that would not combine agreeably with Mr. Johnson's namesake. It sparkles alongside purple salvias. I have a swath of it next to a clump of purple irises, whose spear-shaped foliage contrasts nicely with the geranium's soft form. Both these clumps of geraniums are underplanted with *Allium christophii*, whose great rosy-purple globes hover magically above the foliage.

In early June, the flowers begin to unfurl, nodding sturdily above the leaves. By late June, the plant is a flurry of flowers, though the small size of the blooms and the backdrop of green leaves keep the effect from ever looking clotted. After the first flush, the gardener has two choices—either to cut the plants back hard, after which they will (bolstered by a feeding of foliar fertilizer) put out new clumps of fresh foliage, and, late in the season, a pleasant smattering of blooms; or to do nothing, which is what many gardeners prefer in early July.

If the plants are left alone, they will stretch out, losing some of their tidy shape, and weave instead among other plants, poking stray flowers into the midst of a patch of royal blue *Salvia patens*, for example, or among the glaucous green needles of a *Pinus mugo*, or shinnying up into a rose, from whose branches they will unfurl flowers that startle visitors who think they know a rose blossom when they see one (but suddenly aren't so sure). Either way it is impossible to lose. 'A. T. Johnson' will be among the last plants cut down in the fall.

A geranium I leave alone altogether in the autumn is *G. macrorrhizum* and its kin. Despite claims for other members of the genus, this species is *the* ground-cover geranium, and it truly will blanket the ground, keeping out weeds while providing a handsome fresh foliage through the summer and fall. In addition, *G. macrorrhizum* produces flowers in shades of pink, magenta, and white, depending on the cultivar. The foliage is roughly circular and loosely lobed, and turns handsome shades of red and orange in fall. Perhaps its most striking characteristic is its strong fragrance. (About this fragrance people are much divided—both in description and opinion. Some say it hints of spearmint; others say it reeks of tub cleaner. It reminds me of cedar.) There are tempting hybrids with smaller leaves and refined flowers in muted pinks, but I prefer the straight species, which grows

to 16 inches in good soil and has sharp pink blossoms, a sturdy plant well suited to a life in the
woods.

If it is domesticated blue flowers you crave, the
geranium offers many tempting options. One of
the most notable and sought after is 'Johnson's
Blue,' a plant with elegantly cut foliage and luminous lavender-blue flowers. It is named after the
same A. T. Johnson of the silvery pink plant. Mr.
Arthur Tysilio Johnson, along with his wife, Nora,
had a garden in Wales early in this century, where
he fell under the spell of this genus and did much
to extend its attractions.

Although there are numerous other geraniums
with blue flowers ("blue" being a relative term—
'Johnson's Blue' is described by the Royal Horticultural Society as "violet blue group 94B tinged
with violet blue group 94A, flushed toward the base
of petal with purple group 77A."), the particular
coloring and long season of this hybrid are special.
The plant makes a mound one or two feet tall, with
blue flowers held clear of the foliage. The flowers
are 2 inches across, and their color shines in the

company of old roses and yellow-flowered perennials such as achillea and phlomis.

I have tried roughly two dozen different geraniums in my small garden so far, and have my eye on a half dozen more that sound tempting—striking flower colors, leaves with variegations and interesting patterns. Of the plants I have grown thus far, none has failed to catch my eye and improve my garden in some way. The pelargoniums of the world should feel proud to be mistaken for such a fine group of plants.

SICILIAN CYCLAMENS
by D. H. Lawrence

When he pushed his bush of black hair off
 his brow:
When she lifted her mop from her eyes, and
 screwed it in a knob behind
   —O act of fearful temerity!
When they felt their foreheads bare, naked to
 heaven, their eyes revealed:
When they felt the light of heaven brandished like
 a knife at their defenceless eyes,
And the sea like a blade at their face,
Mediterranean savages:
When they came out, face-revealed, under heaven,
 from the shaggy undergrowth of their own hair
For the first time,
They saw tiny rose cyclamens between their toes,
 growing
Where the slow toads sat brooding on the past.

Slow toads, and cyclamen leaves
Stickily glistening with eternal shadow
Keeping to earth.
Cyclamen leaves

Toad-filmy, earth-iridescent
Beautiful
Frost-filigreed
Spumed with mud
Snail-nacreous
Low down.

The shaking aspect of the sea
And man's defenceless bare face
And cyclamens putting their ears back.
Long, pensive, slim-muzzled greyhound buds
Dreamy, not yet present,
Drawn out of earth
At his toes.

Dawn-rose
Sub-delighted, stone-engendered
Cyclamens, young cyclamens
Arching
Waking, pricking their ears
Like delicate very-young greyhound bitches
Half-yawning at the open, inexperienced

Vista of day,
Folding back their soundless petalled ears.

Greyhound bitches
Bending their rosy muzzles pensive down,
And breathing soft, unwilling to wake to the
    new day
Yet sub-delighted.

Ah Mediterranean morning, when our
    world began!
Far-off Mediterranean mornings,
Pelasgic faces uncovered,
And unbudding cyclamens.

The hare suddenly goes uphill
Laying back her long ears with unwinking bliss.

And up the pallid, sea-blenched Mediterranean
    stone-slopes
Rose cyclamen, ecstatic fore-runner!
Cyclamens, ruddy-muzzled cyclamens

In little bunches like bunches of wild hares
Muzzles together, ears-aprick,
Whispering witchcraft
Like women at a well, the dawn-fountain.

Greece, and the world's morning
Where all the Parthenon marbles still fostered the
    roots of the cyclamen.
Violets
Pagan, rosy-muzzled violets
Autumnal
Dawn-pink,
Dawn-pale
Among squat toad-leaves sprinkling the unborn
Erechtheion marbles.

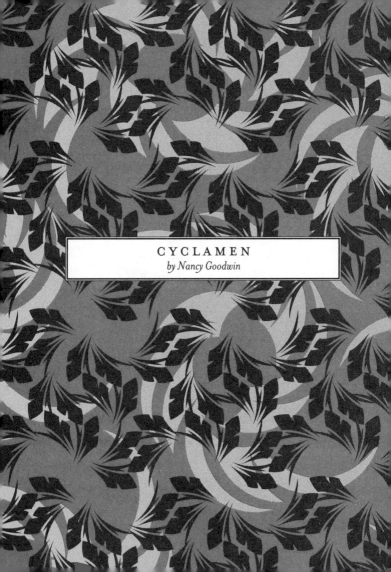

CYCLAMEN
by Nancy Goodwin

I KNOW OF NO OTHER GENUS WHOSE plants flower out-of-doors every day of the year. I know of no other genus with one or more species coming into bloom or growth, peaking or going dormant at every season. Cyclamen is the only one. The rose-purple flowers of *Cyclamen purpurascens* brighten and perfume woodland gardens in summer. *Cyclamen graecum* and *Cyclamen hederifolium* announce the approach of fall with a few flowers in summer and masses of blossoms in September and October. *Cyclamen coum* color the woods with magenta, pink, or white flowers all winter. And *Cyclamen repandum* and *Cyclamen pseudibericum* bloom with pink or white flowers in spring.

Cyclamen aren't grown for their flowers alone. Each plant has a unique pattern of silver or gray leaves, and even the leaf shapes vary from round to ivy-like to sword-like. *C. hederifolium* grow thickly near the large gray rocks in the woods below the formal gardens at my home, Montrose, in North Carolina. *C. coum* clothe another slope nearby. *CC. coum, cilicium, mirabile, pseudibericum, graecum,* and *trochopteranthum* surround a large *Cedrus deodara* near the

front door of the main house. Cyclamen grow in most of the shady beds in my garden, a few in the sunny beds, and one, *C. graecum*, in the scree garden. I have experimented with them, trying them where I knew they would like to grow, where I wanted them to grow, and where I wondered whether they could possibly grow. They survive and thrive in all these places.

I saw my first "wild" cyclamen, *C. hederifolium*, nearly thirty-five years ago, growing in the lawn near a large gray rock in a friend's garden in Surrey. At that time it was the loveliest plant I had ever seen. To this day I have never been more affected by a plant. I couldn't believe it might be hardy enough for me to grow, or that I would know how to nurture it. My husband and I had just purchased our first house in Durham, North Carolina, and I had barely begun my first garden. I wanted to try everything, so I purchased a packet of cyclamen seeds in England and brought them home. After I planted them, I couldn't forget about them, though they germinated and grew with little effort on my part. I visited their part of the garden daily, worrying

about them when they were dormant in summer and rejoicing at the first sight of an incipient bud several months later. I hardly realized that cyclamen would lead me to open Montrose Nursery, the original purpose of which was to propagate and distribute the relatives and descendants of my first plant. My little cyclamen brought me the best friendships I could ever hope to have, and it also finally led me from the music room into the garden, where I have found beauty and peace.

All cyclamen grow from tubers, not from bulbs or corms. They have five petals joined at the mouth, and in most species the petals are flung back like those of their cousins, shooting stars [Dodecatheons]. Only *C. trochopteranthum* and *Cyclamen parviflorum* hold their twisted petals out like propellers. Although most species have downward-facing flowers, occasionally a plant of *C. hederifolium* holds its flowers upside down, with the mouth open to the sky. I have never gotten seed from these plants, probably because the rain destroys the pollen.

When fertilization occurs, the flowers fall off,

leaving a round capsule on a peduncle that coils itself tightly around the developing embryo, pulling it to the ground and protecting it through the winter. When the seed is fully ripe, in late spring or summer, the coil relaxes, the capsule is flabby to the touch, and its tip opens. Ants come quickly and carry off the seeds, eating only the sticky substance surrounding them. This is a wonderful way for the seeds to be dispersed, and within a few years I found plants many feet away from their parents. After twenty years I have mature plants that bloom more than fifty feet away from where I first planted their ancestors. I have immature ones even farther away than that.

My gardening year begins in autumn, for summer in the South is generally as difficult for plants and people as a winter may be in the North. In fall, nights cool off, and gentle, daylong rains replace violent thunderstorms. *C. hederifolium* anticipates the season with a few flowers as early as May, but by September and October there are many. The elegant flowers, some of them fragrant, may be pink or white with tinges of pink, and each has auricles

or little ear-like protuberances at its mouth. By early November we see fewer flowers, as the exquisite and infinitely variable leaves develop. Some of the leaves are shaped, as their name implies, like those of ivy. Others are hastate, or spear-shaped. Most are marked with lighter green or silver. Some are completely silver or pewter-colored, while others have small markings of green along the edges.

By the end of July I find a few plants of *C. graecum* with carmine-pink or pure white flowers open. At a distance these flowers look like those of *C. hederifolium*. But closer examination reveals slender streaks of carmine extending from the mouth to the tips of the petals. The interior of most of the colored flowers is violet. The species has heart-shaped leaves with a velvety sheen and small teeth along the edges. Some leaves may be entirely silver, but most are marked with gray, silver, or lighter green. Each plant has a unique pattern of markings. The tuber of *C. graecum* is markedly different from its relatives; it is corky, with long, thick roots.

A trio of closely related species, *CC. cilicium, mirabile,* and *intaminatum* come into growth in early

fall and persist in flower until well into December. Tiny *C. intaminatum* is one of two miniatures. I grow it on a slope, for to see it properly I must bend to it. Tiny gray lines, invisible at a distance, extend from the mouth to the tips of the palest pink or white petals. The rounded leaves are either entirely green, marked with a few dots of silver, or dramatically patterned in lighter green or silver.

C. mirabile blooms with pink or (very rarely) white flowers; the elegantly twisted petals have fimbriated tips. The angular leaves of some plants are flushed with pink or red when young. *C. mirabile*'s cousin *C. cilicium* is similar in stature but the well-marked leaves are more oblong or spoon-shaped. Small honey-scented flowers, pink to deep carmine, appear in profusion along with or ahead of the leaves. I grow the pure white *C. cilicium* forma *album* just as easily as the more common pink form.

Winter-blooming cyclamen don't wait until the fall-flowering ones finish. *C. coum* comes into leaf in early fall and some buds form by late October. Solid green to silver or pewter leaves vary

in form from round to heart-shaped. The flowers, pure white to darkest magenta, are sometimes fragrant. Unfairly described as dumpy, some of the flowers may indeed be short and fat, but many are elegant and elongated. They appear from November through March, seldom losing leaves or flowers despite severe weather. I have seen perfect blooms after nights of 4°F.

C. parviflorum, the other miniature, also blooms in winter, with tiny, heavily scented flowers and rounded leaves. I grow it next to a path near the metasequoias, where I can kneel and smell its mauve-pink flowers. *C. trochopteranthum* blooms at the same time, with spoon-shaped leaves much like those of *C. cilicium*, but its pink or white petals twist and flare on short stalks.

By the time spring arrives *CC. repandum* and *pseudibericum* are at the peak of their bloom. *C. pseudibericum* has dramatic flowers, the largest of any hardy species, with near-black markings at the base of each petal and a white blotch above. It is slow to come back into growth after the summer but may bloom as early as Christmas. The leaves are more

uniform than those of most species and are generally marked with lighter gray-green patterns. Elegant *C. repandum* has fragrant, pure white or pink flowers and sends up leaves in February and flowers in late February and March, disappearing shortly after that. Its leaves look more consistently like ivy than those of *C. hederifolium*. Pewter-leaved *Cyclamen libanoticum* blooms with large pale pink flowers in a perfect spring, but alas, we seldom have perfect springs. I grow it on a southeast slope; the tubers are hardy, but both flowers and leaves are tender. I now find seedlings nearby, so at least the few flowers that do appear are happy enough to produce seeds. Diminutive *CC. balearicum* and *creticum* bloom in spring, producing new leaves to replace those lost during winter's cold. *C. balearicum* has slender petals faintly lined with pink and gray leaves marked with silver. *C. creticum* has slightly twisted petals, pure white or the palest pink, that are longer than those of *C. balearicum*, and flatter, greener, more ivy-shaped leaves. The flowers of both are scented.

Finally, in late April or May, *C. purpurascens* comes into flower, producing deliciously fragrant, carmine-pink blooms above rounded leaves marked with silver or gray. Some pewter leaves are flushed with purple at the edges. A few plants with pure white flowers grow isolated from the rest. *Cyclamen colchicum* wants the same habitat but produces thick, toothed leaves and flowers shaded to darker carmine at the mouth. I delight in these two species, for I will find their flowers in the garden through the summer, with an occasional one as late as December. New leaves grow in early summer before the old ones disappear, and the seeds from the previous year's bloom ripen just as the fresh flowers open.

The hardiest species seem to be *CC. hederifolium, coum, trochopteranthum, parviflorum, intaminatum, cilicium, colchicum,* and *purpurascens.* These will grow from Zones 8 to 3. *CC. mirabile* and *pseudibericum* are the next hardiest; they will probably grow well into Zone 5. *CC. repandum, creticum, balearicum, libanoticum,* and *graecum* may not be hardy beyond Zone 7. The

tender ones, *CC. africanum, rohlfsianum, persicum, somalense*, and *cyprium*, require the protection of a greenhouse if temperatures dip below 26°F.

I am never in my garden without seeing cyclamen. Usually, about Thanksgiving, when most of my fall chores have been completed and the leaves have fallen from our trees, I walk through the garden and woods in search of young plants. It is like the most splendid game of "follow the dots." I go from one plant to the next in every direction. Cyclamen have crossed the road to the pond. They have gone up the hills and down. I dream of the day when the woods will be carpeted with them. I know that for the rest of my life I will delight in their elegant upswept petals and infinitely variable leaves, and I hope I never lose the feeling of excitement at discovery or rediscovery, as each species returns in its season.

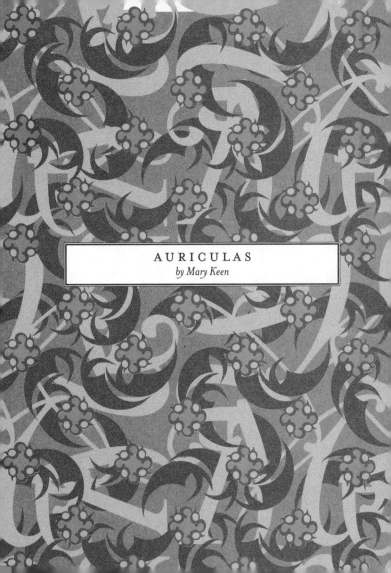

AURICULAS
by Mary Keen

ONCE I MET A MAN WHO WAS, I KNEW, a distinguished grower of rhododendrons on the grand scale. Never having gardened acres of acid soil, I was nervous of drawing him out on his favourite topic. Instead, I said, "Did you see the auriculas at the show last week? Weren't they wonderful?" The Distinguished Grower put down his knife and fork and stared into the space beyond his plate. "One man's meat," he said, "is another man's poison." If you gloat over the ample blowsiness of rhododendrons, the chances are you may not admire auricula. But if, like me, you find rhododendrons overwhelming, rather like fat women dressed to kill, the bright and tidy auricula, like a child with a clean face, may capture your horticultural heart.

Primula auricula was an Alpine flower known to the Romans. The common form has egg-yolk petals and a white eye with a golden pupil at its centre. Unlike its retiring relation, the primrose, it looks such an intelligent flower, with its lively and open face, that you might pass the time of day with it. Early European growers were so besotted with the plants that they bred from this Alpine that they *did* pass days in their company. Lace makers and silk weavers in the northern counties of England traditionally collected and created auriculas in colours that never grew in the Alps, and watched over their progeny with the sort of care that others reserve for their children. Although auriculas can manage frozen winters, they cannot abide the wet, so shelters were arranged to keep them dry and shaded from the sun, almost as though the brightly painted colours might run or fade if exposed to the elements. The eighteenth- and nineteenth-century weavers worked at home and are reported in contemporary accounts to have left their looms several times a day to adjust the position of their pets, whenever the sun or rain threatened.

I cannot pretend such dedication, but part of the appeal of the auricula lies for me in the tradition of their homeliness. These are flowers that have been the intimate companions of people leading modest and often difficult lives. Each time a new colour break appeared, it would have been an occasion of joy. From the sixteenth to the nineteenth century, when the auricula cult was at its height, no sprays existed to fend off pests and diseases, so often a whole collection was wiped out. And then the grower would start all over again. This may not rate as high on the heroic scale as the story of Ernest Wilson, the plant collector who broke his leg in a Tibetan ravine while collecting Regale lilies for subsequent gardeners to grow, but it was a quiet heroism and the personal struggles of the auricula growers deserve some homage.

It is still a struggle to grow the best auriculas. Vine weevils, a twentieth-century evil, are a constant threat. Biological foes will deal with them, but the foes need an even temperature and moist soil to survive long enough to eat the weevils, and this is hard to arrange. If you make the compost wet, the carrot root of the plants can rot, or root aphis might strike, so that woolly collars appear around the precious ones. Root aphis need to be zapped with chemicals, and if sciarid fly comes (also from wet), more zapping is needed, and zapping is what the biological foes cannot take. I keep a watch for the V-shaped bites out of leaves which are a sign of the adult vine weevil, and in the state of permanent paranoia that attends the keeping of the collection, I often mistake pieces of grit for vine weevil grubs. A shed with a glass roof has been constructed for their winter comfort with seven shelves of staging and draughty windows for frost to enter and remind them of their Alpine origins. Each treasure lives in an individual clay pot, $3\frac{1}{2}$ inches across— antiques found in junk shops or hand-thrown by a favourite potter. Getting almost a hundred auriculas through their infant diseases and problems is nerve-racking. Opening and shutting the windows overhead; watering very carefully and only occasionally, with a teapot, so that no water touches any leaf; turning the pots; picking off the dead leaves (with tweezers, the books say), and waiting for the flowers makes winter fly.

Whole books were written about compost and feeding in earlier centuries. All are agreed that a well-drained, gritty, sandy, and leaf-mouldy mixture is best, and that limey soil is what these plants must have. When the flowers start to stir from hibernation, they need a boost, and the question of what to use in spring has always been contentious. Some early growers swore by night soil, others by sheep dung, a few by composted corpses, and one auricular fancier kept three geese especially to feed the plants. Modern growers rely on bottled tonics, but cannot agree on which is best. Anything high in phosphates is good. Opinion is divided about whether to feed or not in summer, because it can hurry the plants into autumn flowering, which is not at all to be encouraged, as it diminishes their spring performance. Happy auriculas produce plantlets from the side of their carrot-shaped roots—sometimes as many as seven from a single plant. All these must be detached and potted. August is a good time for this operation, because the vine weevil grubs can be spotted if they are about and there is less risk of autumn flowers. After they have settled, they have a short spell of growth before falling into winter torpor. No rest for the grower, though. Vigilance is still vital. As the winter closes in, they are moved from the north side of the house, where they sit all summer on the back windowsills, into their own ventilated quarters.

The fuss is all part of the fun. If you grow auriculas, nothing is too good for them. Societies exist for the exchange of information on how best to cosset and pamper the subject of your obsession. Seeds and animadversions reach English growers from across the Atlantic, where conditions are much harsher than they are here. Thomas Jefferson recorded growing auriculas sent from London, and modern collectors in Oregon, British Columbia, Wisconsin, and Virginia are deferred to on this side of the pond. The Fellowship of Fanciers is another good reason for becoming addicted.

As I write, it is November, but my heart gives a lurch of anticipation as I think of April, when the pots on the shelves will each carry a straight stem topped with a tidy flower face. I am new to the game, so my collection has more Alpines than shows (they are easier to grow). Gold-centred 'Sirius,' with an outer ring of apricot-brown petals and an inner ring of mahogany, is a favourite. 'Roweria' has two shades of lilac and a cream centre, 'Sandwood Bay' is crimson and gold, 'Adrian' is blue with a pale cream centre. The Selfs, or single colours, are a notch up from the Alpines. Their centres are pure white with a paste that makes them dazzle. Their petals come in colours seen in the robes of people in Venetian paintings. Clear brilliant reds, like 'Cherry,' or almost blacks, like 'Neat and Tidy.' They are masses of yellow and golds (I like 'Chaiffinch' and 'Chorister'). If the leaves have a serrated edge, I find them even more desirable. Most desirable of all are the green- and grey-edged sorts. See 'Prague' and die. I have only one grey— 'Lovebird'—so far, but my name is down for 'Grey Hawk' and 'Clare.' Fancies are edged with green: I like 'Rajah' and 'Rolts.' The doubles I do not want, but in England growers are breeding stripes again after an interval of a century. I want them. Auriculas make one greedy. I have traveled many miles on hot summer afternoons to fetch some promised varieties that I do not already own. They are plants to dream about and gloat over. The fact that they flower for one spring month matters not a whit to me. I can see the promise in their pointed leaf cones. Their labels, silver on black, are enough to conjure their faces. A faint smell of primrose hangs in the memory. Confined to the smallest of gardens, these are plants that I would be happy to grow for the rest of my life.

BEANS
by Maxine Kumin

LONG AGO IN SUBURBAN BOSTON, when I was but a dilettante gardener, content with a flat of petunias and a few commercially started tomato plants, I first came upon Thoreau's essay "The Bean-Field." *Walden* was part of the core curriculum of freshman English at Tufts University, where I was a part-time instructor, and although my acquaintance with the genus *Phaseolus* was nil, my job required me to pay close attention to the text.

"What shall I learn of beans or beans of me?" Henry David asks. His real concern in this chapter is not with matters of cultivation but with sensuous joys—walking barefoot, observing birds, admiring the emerging wild blackberries. But what overtook him as he hoed his rows was the intrinsic pleasure of his labor, of "making the earth say beans instead of grass."

Forty years later, slave of my garden, I have grown intimate with beans. They are my stars, my best producers, my most versatile charmers. The average bean of our acquaintance originated in South America and was an early explorer export to

❋ ❋ ❋ ❋ ❋ ❋ ❋ ❋ ❋ ❋ ❋ ❋ ❋

Europe in the mid-1600s. Horticulturists have been experimenting with and improving the basic cultivar ever since Gregor Johann Mendel unriddled the secrets of garden peas. The lowly bean comes in a surprising array of possibilities, from compact plants barely a foot high to Jack-and-the-Beanstalk giants. There are half-runners that extend obediently only a foot or so, real runners that wrap around 4-foot stakes, and pole beans for whom the sky is the limit.

I regret that my life will not be long enough to try them all, but I've done some experimenting. In the bush-bean department I've raised Provider, Seville, skinny French flageolet, and flat Romanos planted in triangular clusters down the 3-foot-wide row. Of pole beans, I've enabled yellow and green Kentucky Wonders to hurl themselves up chicken wire or, more recently, fish netting that washed ashore on Cape Cod, where I found great clumps of it on the deserted beach on an autumn vacation. This year, I am raising pole limas with delicate yellow blossoms that will likely not pod up to bear more than a meal or two, though I started them indoors in April, cosseted them through May on the glassed-in front porch, and set them out in the garden on Memorial Day. I have long depended on purple tepee beans, tougher but very hardy, that come to fruition a little later than the green beans and turn a gratifying green when blanched.

I have not yet mentioned scarlet runner beans, whose showy flowers attract hummingbirds, or the hyacinth bean, which was favored by Thomas Jefferson, who had an elaborate arbor constructed for them at Monticello. Scarlet runners and hyacinths both produce edible beans even though they are grown mostly for their flowers. Shelling-out kinds of climbers like Jacob's Cattle beans, Bert Goodwin, black turtle, and cranberry beans will happily twine up any support, including cornstalks, where they will flourish without impeding the ripening ears.

I've tried soybeans, edible in their green phase or allowed to dry for shelling out, but found their flavor no improvement over standard green bean varieties. One year I undertook to raise fava beans, with their purple-spotted white flowers, which grow on the same time schedule as peas, favoring cool weather and good moisture. They are a thick, showy plant and would like to be staked, as they otherwise tend to flop over as they grow. The penny-size beans are a penance to dislodge from their thick and somewhat prickly pods, which form along the length of the stalk; I didn't know at the time that one can blanch them for a minute or two and overcome this difficulty. Some people of Mediterranean heritage are quite allergic to favas. But this bean isn't a bean, after all; it's a vetch, an herb of the genus *Vicia*, that originated in western Asia.

Then there are adzuki beans, of Asian extraction, grown mostly for their edible sprouts, and the asparagus, or yard-long bean, which produces winged pods after its cinnamon-red flowers have gone by. There is the rattlesnake bean, a climber that is bright green with purple stripes, and the horticultural bean. One of the horticultural beans, the Scarlet Beauty Elite, is touted by Pinetree Garden Seeds of Maine as the shell bean that "has outsold Jacob's Cattle beans at the Buckfield General Store," the seeds of which "are amongst the loveliest we have seen, elongated with beautiful shades of purplish brown and beige." A certain eclectic taste is required, I think, to prefer beige and purple beans over more modestly colored ones. Pinetree further says, of Jacob's Cattle, "What Saturday night Bean Supper would be complete without Jacob's Cattle and its remarkable effects on the digestive tract?" (Reading seed catalogues is a wonderful indoor sport!) This bean is sometimes called Trout or Dalmatian bean; New Englanders treasure it because it dries earlier than any other variety, and in our short summers this is a useful attribute.

A friend loaned me a colorful British book on giant vegetables. Following instructions in the text, one can now grow beans over 20 inches long (they will be tough, the author warns). Apparently the cultivation of giant veggies, which began among the Brits, has become a competitive sport; it is slower than cricket and so perhaps more suspenseful. At horticultural shows worldwide such entries are scrupulously inspected and measured. Prizes are given. A gentleman in North Carolina achieved a winning runner bean 48 inches long.

I must say that stretching nature to its limits holds no fascination for me; indeed, I was somewhat horrified to read directions for straightening a bent bean after harvesting. You are directed to tie this miscreant as straight as possible at 3-inch intervals to a strip of wood, wrap the whole package in a damp towel, and leave it alone to think the matter over for twenty-four hours. By then, the bean will have grown somewhat more supple and can be pulled out to its full length. Doesn't this sound like vegetable torture?

Almost any old beans can be grown for the seeds inside the pods, much as we grow English, or shelling-out, peas. Even unintentionally forgotten beans, weary beans you didn't get around to picking in time, will yield bean seeds that are delicious fresh, especially when braised with garlic and minced onion. Dried, they can be displayed in glass jars until the snowy February day you decide to make a thick bean soup.

Some modest planning ahead is required. Dried beans need to soak overnight before going into the cooking pot, along with everything else you have on hand. An all-day simmer fills the house with a tantalizing aroma worth, as they say, half the candle. By this time it may be blizzarding and the power may have gone out, so that you will need all the candles you have providentially stored up. But if you're an addicted vegetable gardener you develop this sort of storing-up personality: dried beans in jars, herbs in the cupboard, blanched vegetables enough to feed a battalion down cellar in the freezer.

Pests aren't much of a problem on beans in my garden. The dread Japanese beetle will move on from the raspberry patch to attack the uppermost leaves of pole beans late in the season. I handpick these copper-backed beasts and shake them off into a can filled with soapy water. Growing some sweet peas alongside beans encourages pollinating insects, I am told, and these in turn should discourage the evil kind. I am a great advocate of spray made from the Indian neem tree, now certified as safe for edibles as well as flowers and shrubs. It does not interfere with the action of the beneficials, those insects, like parasitic wasps, that interrupt the reproductive cycle of the invaders.

I confess nothing looks prettier to me than a well-tended flourishing vegetable garden. Raised beds, mown or mulched walkways, and an attractive fence all around impose the discipline and order that are in short supply in my somewhat chaotic life. Once, I didn't know beans about beans. Now I am a bean counter and proud of it.

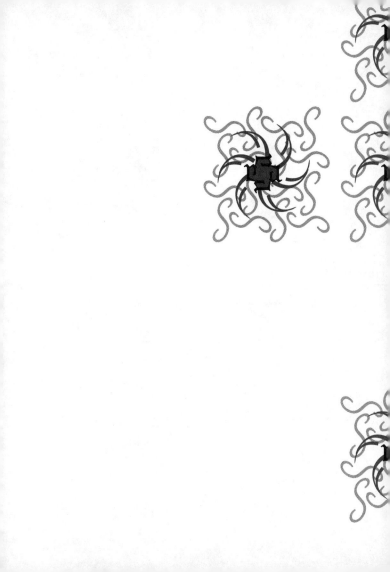

A DAY ON THE EDGE
OF THE WORLD

by F. Kingdon Ward

I AM SITTING BY THE FIRE IN MY LOG hut in the Seinghku valley. A keen wind is blowing through the chinks and crannies, but wrapped in a long woollen *chupa*, by the fire, sipping a nightcap of rum and hot water, I do not feel the cold. From outside comes only the shrill voice of the stream bubbling over the stones, and the occasional clatter of falling rocks high up on the screes; otherwise it is very still. By ten o'clock I am yawning, and having written up my diary, I prepare to turn in. But first I take a look round outside to see that all is well. The fine mist which usually fills the air after dark has disappeared and the sky is riddled with stars. Far down the valley a scimitar moon is being withdrawn slowly from a scabbard of cloud. "Tomorrow it will be fine," I say to myself, stamping my feet, for at 11,000 feet altitude it is chilly at night even in July, and there is much snow higher up the valley; "I will go for a big climb"; and with that pleasant thought I crawl between the blankets and snuggle down for the night.

At six o'clock next morning Chokara comes in and lights the fire, above which, on a bamboo rack, paper, clothes, and bundles of specimens are drying in the smoke. Laphai follows with coffee and hot chapatis. "It is a fine day, *Duar*," says he, and adds that Maung Ba, my cook, is sick with fever. I get out of bed with a shudder, fling on a *chupa*, gulp some scalding coffee, and begin to dress—shorts, a warm flannel shirt, woollen jacket, two pairs of thick socks, and well-nailed climbing boots. While breakfast is being brought in—porridge and curried chicken today—I prepare for the climb.

The botanist need never burden himself with much apparatus in the field. A bag for plants is better than the metal vasculum sold to budding botanists in England; one or two tobacco tins are carried in the pocket for very small specimens, and a biscuit tin may be taken as well for fragile flowers. Fieldglasses, a pocket lens for resolving doubtful points quickly with fresh material, a notebook and pencil, a compass, a strong knife, a pair of Rolcut secateurs for cutting prickly shrubs and the tough stems of rhododendrons, and some string—the sort of miscellania a schoolboy might cram into his pocket—completes the list. A lunch ration consisting of several biscuits, a few raisins or figs, and a slab of chocolate is also taken, more in case of accident than to be eaten at a fixed hour.

I call Chokara and issue final instructions. "Change the plant paper and get my clothes dried. Tell Laphai to take the gun and see if he can shoot a pheasant. Have tea ready for me when I return." Then I go across to the men's hut and have a look at Maung Ba, who is rolled up like a cocoon by the fire. Some medicine is prepared for him and I depart; one advantage of living simply is that if my cook does go sick, anyone else can make curry and rice for me, brew tea or coffee, and fry chapatis. All the same it *would* be nice to start off one morning on a breakfast of kidneys and bacon and hot buttered toast, or perhaps a fried sole and a mushroom omelette . . . One can have great fun making up imaginary menus!

And now, which way shall we go? Up the main valley or up the branch valley? The former leads to the Diphuk La; the latter, which recently was filled with mountainous masses of snow, leads to an enclosure, surrounded by high bare cliffs, with snow beds in the topmost valleys. As soon as the snow is softened by warm winds and rain in May blowing up from the jungle, avalanches begin to slip down the steep gullies and pile up vast heaps in the main valley, which in the middle of June is still snowbound, though the flanks are by then stripped clean. But the torrents of icy water which come rushing down the gullies and the cascades which cleave in a film to the cliffs prevent direct access to the high peaks; and as for the screes, falling stones are a constant menace.

However, on this occasion, I decided to go up the branch valley, past the highest clump of fir trees and the tall granite cliff over which hung a ribbon of white water. There was a cattle path above the furious torrent, which led to a cluster of bothies about two miles up the valley; but the yak had not yet eaten their way as high up as this.

I walked fast at the start, both to get warm and because I was anxious to reach a new hunting ground high up. Anyone set down in this country for the first time would have found a score of flowers to beguile him in the first hundred yards; indeed, no botanist who was a complete stranger to this part of the world would have got half a mile from camp that day, so overwhelmed would he have been with the marvellous wealth of alpine vegetation all round him. Picture the scene! A steep glen is enclosed by mountains rising for 3,000 feet above the foaming torrent. Massive cliffs rise bluntly on one side, stone chutes, wide at the base, but tapering for a thousand feet to where a sword cut gapes in the brow of the mountain, slope up on the other. Ahead, the domed bulk of a granite mountain on the main watershed dominates the glen; and everywhere there is snow. The furious torrent dashes over the rocks with a roar, and the tinkle of water falling over the edge of the world into the main valley is heard. The narrow path, which frequently twists to avoid enormous blocks of stone, is lined with bushes, mostly species of rhododendron. A dense scrub clings round the base of the cliff; and on the banks and rocks are primulas, poppies, anemones, the yawning violet mouths of *Omphalogramma souliei*, purple morina, clusters of yellow saxifrage, frail veronica, pink

Nomocharis, and a great many more flowers. But I had been ten days at River Camp already, and most of these flowers I knew well. Many of them I had seen before, in the Himalaya or in China; I was pleasantly aware that beautiful flowers surrounded me on every hand. Was it not enough that I was filled with the quiet joy of living amidst glorious scenery—it was glorious when it was visible—breathing the keen mountain air, and feeling fit to keep going for ten hours, or twenty if necessary, and to climb to any height likely to be reached by plant life!

But I had not gone far when my attention was drawn to a dwarf iris, whose stemless flowers opened, as it seemed, straight out of the ground. They grew singly or in clumps of two or three, on a turf slope, sodden from melting snow. I dug up several plants and placed them in a tin; next day when I opened the tin, there was a delicious scent as of fresh greengages, but this was too delicate and refined to be noticeable in the open. This bulbous iris was quite rare, and in fact I saw it nowhere else in the valley. I therefore made special efforts to

collect seed of it in October and discovered about a
dozen capsules, only just appearing above the surface of the soil. Two years later, in the Mishmi
Hills, I found the same plant again. Here it was
much more abundant, forming large solid clumps,
sometimes with a dozen or more flowers in each;
though one was lucky to find a single ripening capsule where there had been a dozen flowers!

The same grassy slope which produced the
dwarf iris was speckled with the mop heads of a
pigmy primula, *P. genestieriana*. This neat little plant
draws itself up to its full stature of half an inch on
the rhododendron moorland at 14,000 to 15,000
feet, and bursts into a puffball of tiny flowers,
which may be pink, purple, or violet. I took endless
trouble to collect seed of the minute creature, but it
was all wasted energy, for the plant refused to grow
in England, and is too small to be of much account
if it did!

After that I came to hillsides covered with a
mixed heath of dwarf rhododendron, especially the
purplish pink *R. riparium* and the larger *R. saluenense*,
with flat Tyrian-purple flowers and glistening

bands of silver scales on their backs. Mixed with these was one of the aromatic "Cephalanthum" rhododendrons, a taller and more erect plant, dabbled over with compressed heads of tiny pink flowers, like blobs of sea foam.

A large bush rhododendron which I named Cherry Brandy (*R. cerasinum*) overhung the torrent, and was particularly lovely when wet. It had pendent bells of a bright cherry red, with cream rim, in trusses of five or six, and looked like a fruit salad. The rather rounded leaves are smooth beneath, except for a coating of wax, as seen in *R. thomsonii*. In Tibet in 1924 I had collected the same plant, the flowers like red garnets, with five jet-black circular pit glands at the base. It grows also in the Mishmi Hills, where it sometimes has carmine flowers; but the cherry and cream variety from the Seinghku is probably the handsomest.

By this time I was clear of the larger scrub, and glancing up the screes, I was just in time to see a flower twinkle, as a bayonet of sunlight stabbed the clouds. Approaching, I stood in silent wonder before the ruby poppy. In Sino-Himalaya, the mountain poppies are generally blue, sometimes yellow, very rarely red. Therefore a red poppy here is as exciting as a blue poppy in England. Also it was exquisite. A sheaf of finely drawn olive-green jets shot up in a fountain from amongst the stones, curled over, and, ere they reached the ground again, splashed into rubies. Thus one might visualise *Meconopsis rubra*, if one imagines a fountain arrested in mid-career, and frozen. But it was not till later, when on a stormy day I saw whole hillsides dotted with these plants, that I really believed in *M. rubra*. As the wind churned up the clouds, a burning brand was lit, and touched off the flowers one by one; up they went in red flame! That was convincing. The ruby poppy! I thought, what a plant for the rock garden! But then, of course, it won't grow in England!

And so on up the valley, over beds of snow, across frothing streams, in a wilderness of meadow flowers rioting over a carpet of rhododendron. There were sky-blue poppies and yellow primulas, pink and red *Nomocharis*, several kinds of pedicularis, monk's hood, trollius, the silken white *Anem-*

one wardii, and—yes! golden anemone! In stature and foliage this last is very like *A. wardii*, and in fruit I could not tell them apart; and yet in flower it has these brazen yellow discs, just as *Meconopsis rubra* is practically *M. impedita* with blood-red flowers. But *M. rubra* grew everywhere, and there was no true blue *M. impedita* in the Seinghku valley; whereas the golden anemone grew just here and here only; everywhere else it was replaced by the far more abundant white anemone.

Reaching the bothies at an altitude of 12,000 to 13,000 feet, I found myself on a hillock, clearly an ancient moraine, through which the torrent broke, to fall over a ledge into the valley below. Beyond this, streams wandered across a wide sandy flat, amongst small bushes of rhododendron and willow. All around, the screes slanted up steeply for hundreds of feet, and at the head of the basin, a low cliff, its edge bevelled by the scour of ice, blocked the valley. Above that again was a smaller amphitheatre, floored with moraine material and surrounded by straight bare cliffs.

The broom-like rhododendron which grew in

the sand was capped all over with tight heads of flowers of so dusky a purple that in the shadow they looked like royal mourning; in the sunlight, however, they became a daring plum-juice colour which glowed amongst the frosted leaves. It is *R. rupicola*, one of the "Lapponicum" rhododendrons, dwarf or brushwood plants with very small crisp leaves and flowers which display perhaps a greater variety of colours than any other group in the genus; in fact, almost any colour, except red or orange. Nor are the flowers ever spotted or blotched.

Meanwhile, I had not been idle. A number of plants had been transferred to my bag or into one or other of the tins. I had noticed the type of rock met with, the various plant associations, and the general features of the valley, down which once upon a time a glacier had flowed. I recorded those plants which were rare or local, confined to certain gullies or cliffs, and those which were common everywhere. All this was intensely interesting; I only lacked a companion with whom I could share these delights.

Whither should I go now? Should I continue up the main valley or ascend the scree and try to reach one of the hanging valleys? I chose the latter, because that would bring me out on the open top, where I could wander about more freely and perhaps enjoy a view. Presently I found myself in a steep gulley, choked with enormous rocks. I had great difficulty in surmounting some of these obstacles, since there was always the danger of pulling the rock down on me as I hauled myself up, if it happened to be insecurely perched.

Now I noticed a very curious thing. As I ascended towards the crest of the main watershed which separates the Irrawaddy from the Lohit the climate became drier. Even the flora showed this. More conclusive was the weather, which I could see for myself improved towards the top of the valley. On several occasions afterwards, both in June and July when climbing above 13,000 feet, in bright sunshine, I looked back, like Lot's wife, and saw a pillar of cloud by day hanging over my camp. But the mist bank stopped short there at 11,000 feet, as though held back by some invisible barrier—really the dry air sweeping over the pass off the plateau. It was this mist bath which prevented the melting of the enormous heaps of snow in the lower valley and kept the air so cold.

The range then was a climatic barrier of the first importance—was, in fact, itself part of the great rain screen which separates the wet hills of the frontier from the dead heart of Asia. I was already on the edge of the drier region and might reasonably expect to find a different flora on the other side of the pass.

The gulley now grew steeper and narrower, and presently ended in a chimney, up which I scrambled, to find myself in a hanging valley, with a small lake at its head. At the foot of an escarpment was a boulder-strewn slope which dipped gently down to the lake stream. Beyond the lake, its base hidden by a fold in the ground, was a sugarloaf peak, about 17,000 feet high; and on its flank lay a snow bed.

It was a glorious flower-spangled valley, tucked away here on the crest of the range. Long ago it had clasped a glacier, but all that remained of it were these snow beds, cowering in the topmost hollows and dwindling year by year. A larger glacier, fed from several of these hanging valleys, had flowed down the big valley up which I had come, past my camp, where it had joined the main ice stream from the Diphuk La; and the combined stream had flowed on down the valley to Snowy Camp, just below which it had ended.

What had brought about this profound change? Climatic revolution? There was no means of knowing. But in those days, when the valleys were filled with ice, there could have been no alpine flowers here. On the other hand, forest may have prevailed at higher levels than it does now; for the climate was probably moister, which would have favoured tree growth. In Tibet, many glaciers in the Tsangpo gorge descend far below the tree line to this day. In the Seinghku valley isolated clumps of trees, fir and larch, survive on sheltered slopes and ancient moraines some distance above the general timberline; and these appear to be outliers of more extensive forests, dating from a moister age, rather than pioneers which have recently established themselves. In this age an alpine climate is in the ascendant, and it is the forest which is being forced back; the great amount of smashed timber, often buried in the gravel and silt washed down the mountain, is good evidence for that. The glaciers are still retreating all over Sino-Himalaya—in the eastern Himalaya, in Tibet, in the Burmese Oberland, in western China, everywhere; they have been retreating for a long, long time. They may even have retreated farther, and faster, on the inner dry ranges than on the outer wet ranges. No one knows why they are retreating; in fact, hardly anyone knows of the existence of all these glaciers and vanished glaciers! As they retreat, the alpine flora advances, and the forest is cut off or pushed back. This matter of former glaciation is of particular interest to the botanist, because it helps to throw light on the distribution of plants in Sino-Himalaya.

In the midst of these thoughts, suddenly I noticed that the ground under my feet was soft with the cushions of a primula which resembled a large violet-flowered primrose. Unfortunately, this distinct species, *P. chamœthauma*—Wonder of the Snow—belongs to a group, alien to Europe, which obstinately refuses to grow at sea level, even in Britain; and despite its resemblance to a primrose (which is more imaginary than real) and a fat packet of seed which I collected, *P. chamœthauma* is not in cultivation. Like the beautiful and elusive *Primula sonchifolia*, the seeds germinated, soon to perish miserably; and the only species of the "Petiolaris" section which remains somewhat precariously in cultivation is *P. winteri.*

P. chamœthauma is extremely abundant in the high alpine valleys of the Seinghku, above 13,000 feet—though it may be found as low as 12,000 feet. It is gregarious, and I saw more than one turf slope absolutely violet with its cabbage leaves and massive heads. A single plant I noticed had white flowers.

On patches of gravel, carefully avoided by *P. chamœthauma*, the exquisite Claret Cup (*Primula silaensis*) grew in scores. It is about an inch high, its stem as fine as thread, and its wine-purple bellflowers hang singly or in pairs, rarely in threes. The spoon-shaped leaves form a neat rosette on the ground, from which rises the fairy staff, with the red bell swinging by a ligament from its apex. This is one of the most charming of the amethystina or jewel primulas. They are almost entirely unknown in England, except in the anhydrous state.

Several large chunks of rock, broken off the cliff above, had rolled down the slope here, and the alpine flowers had already healed the scars. One was a complete rock garden in miniature. Against a blood-red film of scarlet runner (*Rhododendron repens*), the violet stars of little *Primula bella* twinkled brightly, and soft purple clouds of *Primula bryophila* flung pale shadows over the constellations. The thought struck me, why not have a rock garden of my own in camp? There were several enormous erratic blocks which had been carried down the valley by the glacier and dumped close to my log hut; nothing would be easier than to convert one of them into a rock garden, where I could cultivate any number of high alpines. The advantages of such a scheme were twofold. Small alpines which grow by themselves in isolated gullies and on remote cliffs, however conspicuous in flower, are very easily passed over when out of flower; add to this that in October they might be under snow and not merely invisible but unapproachable, and the advantage of moving them to a place of safety becomes obvious. In the second place, to have them on the spot in the autumn, seeding into my hand, so to speak, would save much unnecessary climbing. I therefore resolved that in future, whenever I found a tiny alpine of which I required seed, I would dig up a certain number of plants, carry them back to my camp, and plant them in my garden as a reserve. In fact, I did this, transporting plants of *Primula rhodochroa*, Claret Cup, and Blue Microbe (*Primula fea*), all of them exquisitely minute. They all set seed, but not one of them is in cultivation now—I do not think any of them even flowered, nor had they done so would anyone but the most enthusiastic rock gardener, or a botanist, waste a thought on them. They are too minute; one almost requires a pocket lens to see them at all! It is only when, like Claret Cup, they grew in such countless thousands that you could not set foot on the slope without crushing dozens; or when, like Blue Microbe, they haunted the highest, starkest cliffs, where nothing else could or would grow, that one became aware of them at all. These jewel flowers will not grow under any conditions we have so far been able to devise for them in this country.

I now scaled the cliff and found myself looking over into the next valley. Descending into that, I walked up a slope rich with meadow flowers, all the time keeping a sharp lookout for the rare or unknown plant. *Primula serratifolia* grew here in clumps; also several species of Lloydia, with white or egg-yellow flowers, *Bergenia*, saxifrages, globeflower, pedicularis, and a fritillaria. And presently I came on what I sought—a plant quite new to me. From a nest of narrow-toothed, softly hairy leaves sprang a white powdered stem, 6 inches high, ending in a poker head of powder-blue narrow tubular flowers. It was *Primula wattii*, one of the "Soldanella" primulas, so called from some resemblance to *Soldanella alpina*, a plant often seen flowering in the snow on the mountains of Europe. This is the first record of *P. wattii* outside Sikkim, 400 miles to the west; and its unexpected discovery so far east filled me with delight. Another interesting fact was that some days before, I had found two white-flowered primulas on a fresh earth slip, about 2,000 feet below this. I was curious to know what they were, and had hunted high and low for more plants, without success; and now at last I had found them 2,000 feet higher up on the same slope—*Primula wattii*! Evidently these two plants had sprung from seed which had been carried far down the slope by some casual agency, and had lived to flower; but why were they white instead of blue? It did them no service, for I marked both plants carefully, and neither set a single seed! *P. wattii* was not common. The plants were widely scattered over the grassy slope, and in a side glen I found some more; nowhere else did I see a single plant. I worked like a horse—or a chamois—collecting seed of this plant in October, but the plants raised did not prosper.

Above me an overhanging brow of rock cut right across the face of the mountain, and was carved into a series of towers. Beyond this the ridge climbed in lame steps up the escarpment beneath an immensity of scree. On the grey grass cliffs, strung out in flights along the fissures, was Blue Microbe (*P. fea*), an elfin primula so wee that the

threadlike stem will pass through the eye of a needle, while the pagoda bellflower is no larger than a
brownie's cap. This bell is crimson at the base,
changing to blue above, and is hung from the stem
by the finest silken cord. Two, sometimes three,
bells nod on each stem—no more. So much for
P. fea, another homeless orphan; but the frail
beauty of this gem is almost as apparent in the dried
specimen as it is in the living plant.

Searching for plants no larger than this is like
looking for ore in a rock. They seem to have crystallised out of the grey magma. At a distance of a few
yards, they are quite invisible in cracks and crannies where nothing else grows. From the hum-
mocky turfed steps fluttered the green ribbon
leaves of *P. bryophila*, and a few thorny barberry
bushes crouched between the rocks. The talus
tipped from the crags here overflowed the ridge,
and at a height of about 14,000 feet I found myself
walking on a firm snow crust, where ridge and scree
rolled hand in hand to the foot of the final
precipice. From this point I turned my steps down-
hill towards camp, thinking mainly of tea and dry

clothes. The day was far spent. What did it matter to me that I had in my bag several beautiful plants never seen before by man, besides others, which, if not actually new, were so in effect? Several of these, could I but introduce them into Britain, would elicit a chorus of "Oh's" and "Ah's" at the Chelsea Flower Show. Did not that mean fame? A temporary notoriety perhaps! But did that matter now? No, certainly not. What mattered now was that I was tired, cold, and hungry; I wanted to rest and I wanted some hot tea. But sheer force of habit made me keep a good lookout for plants as I followed the ridge between the two glens, and presently dropped into a gulley.

Meanwhile, I mused on the day's work, and especially on *Primula wattii*. As I have said, it was not a new species, but its discovery here was of peculiar interest. How did it get here? It did not suddenly appear in two places 400 miles apart. It must have travelled along the mountain ranges between, though under existing conditions it could not do so. Conditions then must have changed. We have seen, for instance, that the whole of this region was once buried under ice, which has since disappeared. That probably takes us far enough back in time for our purpose. But long before that, there must have been great movements of the earth's crust, since the sedimentary rocks have been bent in all directions, buckled, flung up on edge, and crystallised.

The central core of mountains comprising Sino-Himalaya have a peculiar structure. The high peaks stick up here and there abruptly like rocky islands from an ocean floor; the surrounding alpine slopes are as smooth, undulating, and easy as the surface of a calm sea. Here one can wander without hindrance, anywhere above 14,000 feet. Far below in deep troughs the torrents plunge and roar, and as you descend towards them, you notice the slope steepen more and more sharply until finally it breaks off in a sheer cliff. It is this bulge in the slope which prevents you from seeing the high peaks on either side as you march up the main valley; the peaks lie far back, and what look like the summits of mountains against the sky are really nothing but a row of stacks marking the shoulder where the slope suddenly eases off onto the ice shelf—all that remains of the ancient plateau.

The simple explanation of this structure is that the whole mountain country was originally a plateau, like the plateau of Tibet, of which it still forms an outlying part. At that time it was under ice, and wide shallow valleys lay between one range and the next; the flanks of those valleys were the rolling slopes across which we have been wandering, where today flowers blow.

As the glaciers shrank, the streams cut ever deeper into the rock, while the uplands were still preserved beneath a coat of snow, and when the ice finally disappeared, water quickly completed the task of cutting deep and narrow grooves in the plateau. The structure of the country is conclusive on this point. It is the same in Tibet, in western China, in the Himalaya, in Burma, and in Assam. If other evidence were needed, it will be found in the plants themselves. The ancient plateau, that is to say, the ice shelf, which is all that remains of the plateau, has a flora quite different from that of the valleys. It is this highly specialised plateau flora which alone invites comparison with the Arctic flora; and it is not too much to say that no plant which grows habitually on the ice shelf will be hardy in Britain. English weather will on the whole satisfy the average alien from a temperate climate, but the specialist plant from the hot desert or the cold desert or the 100 percent saturated atmosphere cannot brook it. Even plants like primula and meconopsis, which belong to hardy genera, fail completely with us if they come from the plateau. We cannot grow any of the "Amethystina" primulas, and the "Rotundifolia" are almost as bad. *Primula minor, P. dryadifolia, P. fea, P. rhodochroa, P. bella*, and others have all been tried and found wanting. *Meconopsis speciosa, M. impedita, Wardaster lanuginosus* (the flannel-leafed aster of Muli), *Myosotis hookeri*, and *Campanula calcicola*, all typical plateau plants, have fared no better.

Despite their proximity, even contact, plateau flora and valley flora remain distinct. It is not merely a matter of altitude. These plants, which must have inhabited the plateau ever since it was freed of ice, have a different constitution. Several of them are widely distributed between the Karakorum and western China, e.g., *Potentilla peduncularis, Anemone polyanthes, Myosotis hookeri, Braya sinensis, Draba alpina.*

So much for my thoughts as I slid and slithered back to camp.

But during much of the time one is engaged in thinking of less romantic things—food and warmth and sleep, for instance, and the mere routine of carrying on. One must needs be not only self-contained but self-reliant. Should any of the men fall sick, one turns doctor; should they quarrel or steal, one turns J.P. One may also be called upon to cook, to interpret, to mend apparatus, or in short to do any odd job, besides collecting, examining, and describing specimens. Above all, one's servants have to be fed and looked after in a country where they cannot buy food for themselves.

Most people find it difficult to sleep at altitudes much greater than those to which they are accustomed. Many suffer from insomnia as low as 6,000 feet, though personally I am not affected below about 10,000 feet.

In times of acute depression one harks back to a previous existence, and lets the mind browse on memories: the conversation of friends, music, the theatre, gardens, and holiday crowds. Movement, events; here things happen with the gigantic inertia of geological epochs. One even dares to look forward to a time when one will enjoy such phantasias again. Possibly it is only a harmless delusion that these things have anything to do with life at all: but if so, most of us happily share that delusion. After all, these are the things one was brought up to reckon with; whereas romantic scenery, adventure, the violence of nature, and playing a lone hand were rare fruits to be tasted judiciously, not swallowed whole. Those who envy the plant hunter his free, careless life are apt to forget this; they forget that he has renounced many of the things which make life pleasant. He may have chosen the wiser part; and at any rate he *had* the choice, a choice which falls to few men. But people who envy him are often thinking of the results rather than of the slow and usually painful steps which led to those results. The only existence they know of which can be compared with the plant hunter's life is their own annual summer holiday, when for a short time they can turn their back on the shams and formalities of civilisation and shun all men except one or two boon companions. And if the weather is bad, how bored they are! But at the end of a fortnight in the wilds, how many men would be willing to stay on? Some, of course; probably not many. After all, do we not enjoy a change just because it *is* a change? Even the most exhilarating holiday palls at last, and we are glad to return to our accustomed bondage, to see the friends we are used to, to do the safe everyday things once more! Though we are not aware of it, our dislike of solitude is at bottom *fear*, and we seek the society of our fellow creatures because in the midst of the herd we feel *safe*. It seems easier to die in the sunlight, and together, than in the darkness, alone, as wild beasts die. Plant hunting, then, may be a wonderful life, but it certainly is not the life most men picture it to be. It is a life's work, and like all work worthy of the name, it involves responsibility and toil. However, let us drop philosophy and continue our scramble.

To descend an unexplored gulley connecting the ice shelf with the main valley is to risk trouble. Sooner or later the gulley will end in a cliff. However, on this occasion I had no difficulty, and presently found myself on a tall scree, with a straight descent into the valley. On the scree I noticed tuffets of a dwarf rhododendron, with pairs of pale pink flowers borne stiffly on long stalks. The plants were scattered, never forming a continuous carpet like most of the dwarf rhododendrons, though that might have been the fault of the scree. This was Pink Baby (*R. pumilum*), a plant of the eastern Himalaya. So absorbed was I with this find that I did not at first notice several other remarkable plants on the scree. There was in fact a threadbare carpet of dwarf undershrubs, including willow and honeysuckle, clinging in strips to the otherwise naked surface, and woven into it were two plants of great charm. The first was a species of gaultheria, whose flowers were so small as to be scarcely visible; the other a creeping rowan (pyrus). But it was not till the autumn, when I saw both plants in fruit, that I realised how good they were. By that time the wee flowers of the gaultheria had given place to large "berries" of a pure and delicious rose colour; and the short flowering stems which grew stiffly upright, like sprigs of moss, crowded with needle leaves, bore many rosy "berries." *G. procumbens*, which is common on mossy banks in the fir forest, and *G. nummularioides*, which is found in drier country, are rather similar in habit, but more prostrate; also the "berries" of the former are bright cyanide blue, those of the latter black. As for the pyrus, its numerous clusters of reddened berries presently turned snow white, beading the crinkly black stems with moonstones.

Descending the scree now as quickly as possible, I reached the path in the valley up which I had started in the morning and, pushing through the rhododendron bushes, hastened down to my hut. Chokara was waiting for me. There was a bright fire burning; my pyjamas, solignified with the wood smoke of weeks, were warm; and seating myself, I let Chokara unlace my boots while I stripped off my wet shirt. Then Laphai appeared with the table-cloth, and by the time I had changed into dry clothes, tea was steaming on the table. The plants were laid out on the bed and forgotten for half an hour, while I drank cup after cup of foaming hot tea and ate toasted chapatis.

I have mentioned a dozen plants found during a typical day's work, but it is obvious that one cannot always be finding new species. There must be *some* limit, over a limited area; sometimes several days pass without a single new plant being added to the collection. Why is this plant so common and that one so rare? How do all these new species come to be here, and here only? Why are they not also like the majority, found either in Sikkim to the west or Yunnan to the east? During the long days of wandering, as one looks at the scenery, the flowers, and the rocks, these and many other problems present themselves for solution; but the answers do not come while you wait, neither in the excitement of the climb nor in the quiet of the hut, nor in the long, often sleepless hours of night. Not that day, nor the next, nor perhaps at any time. One sees and records. And yet an answer to some minor problem, or a working hypothesis which will cover a host of observed facts, may leap into the mind at any moment, anywhere.

But during the actual climbing, you *must* concentrate on what you are doing, and think *ahead*, or disaster is certain. I do not now mean climbing in the technical sense of climbing a chimney or crossing a glacier, but being out on these mountains at all, especially alone. Direction, rock and snow surfaces, and above all weather have to be reckoned with. There is no morning paper with its weather forecast; but that is of no consequence. You can easily forecast it yourself, because it is always either unsettled or downright bad. Plant hunting rarely involves serious climbing; mostly it is marching and scrambling. But the risk of losing one's way, or of being injured by falling rocks, or tumbling over a cliff, or getting into a fix, is an ever-present menace. Of course, such risks become a part of your life; you do not think of them, though common prudence makes you careful. Your aim is to be bold, but not rash; cautious, but not fearful. Again, the sheer physical labour of climbing day after day and week after week above 12,000 feet in a country where the earth's crust is on edge dulls the senses. One's impressions are neither so numerous nor so vivid as they become in stimulating society; nor, on the other hand, are they so fleeting. Yet whatever the dangers and hardships of the plant hunter's life, he too has his reward. Often and often I have stood in a friend's garden in England looking at some child of the snows, glowing with health and vigour, which had taxed me to the uttermost farthing, and said to myself: "It was worth it!"

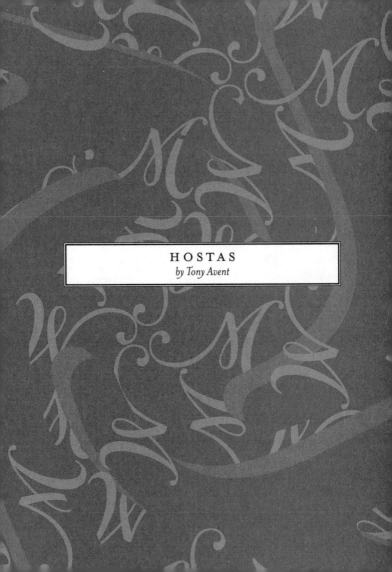

HOSTAS
by Tony Avent

ONE OF MY EARLIEST RECOLLECTIONS is growing up with hostas in the garden. It didn't seem to matter how many times I rode my bicycle through those clumps along the driveway, they kept coming back . . . Indeed, they proved tougher than I. Little did I know that the plants I tried to destroy as a kid would become my lifelong addiction.

Of all the people who have grown hostas for years, there are always those who believe there are exactly two varieties: the green and the variegated. I vaguely believed this, too, until at the ripe old age of nine my folks took me to Raleigh to visit the nationally renowned home gardener Jim Cooper. This person was really strange, I thought, since he grew over fifty different varieties of hosta, which in 1966—in the days before every gardener was a breeder—even I knew was a lot. Of course, at age nine, a garden big enough to run and jump in thrilled me more than the hostas growing in it, but still, I couldn't get them out of my mind.

Each successive trip to Cooper's garden found me spending more time with notepad in hand, slowly walking around the beds trying to memorize all the hosta names (having already mastered the states and their capitals). Being a generous sort, and the unofficial ambassador of hosta, Cooper was always free with a division of anything that struck my fancy, although I was aghast when he told me that some hostas cost as much as $100 per plant. Should I call the mental hospital, I secretly wondered, or do other people find it natural to spend an entire car payment on one plant?

My first hosta was the common variegated kind, 'Undulata.' It is tough as nails, divides easily, grows fast, but it sure is ugly! I don't know why anyone would ever buy another hosta after growing this dog. Okay, in spring it looks great as it emerges from its winter sleep, but it picks up ugly again pretty quickly. Even the flowers are so ugly that I was taught from an early age to run and cut them as soon as I saw the bloom stalks forming. I figured it must be like looking at Medusa's head. If I caught a glimpse of a hosta flower, I would turn into something horrible . . . like a kudzu vine.

There were several different *H.* 'Undulata' type

hostas or subvarieties on the market, and being a collector wannabe, I searched for them all. There was an all-green one called 'Undulata Erromena' . . . the "undulata mistake." Then came 'Undulata variegata' and 'Undulata Univittata,' and 'Undulata White Ray,' all of which proved to be the same when grown under the same conditions. Only the attractive 'Undulata Albomarginata' turned out to be worth the trouble, and the rest were abandoned after a few years. I quickly realized that so-called collectors collected plant names and were not often interested in good garden plants.

I next moved on to the *Hosta* 'Fortunei' group, from which many of the truly good garden hostas have been derived. They include the wonderful old favorite 'Francee.' Not only is it easy to grow and carefree, but the color doesn't fade as with *H.* 'Undulata.' I later would meet dozens of good nurserymen who had perpetuated the myth that hostas hate fertilizer, and that it makes them turn green. I would explain to each of them that 'Undulata' naturally turns green (a process called viridescence), and that fertilizer only hastens the process. This is certainly not true of other, better cultivars and is only one of many garden myths.

Another of my early acquisitions was 'Gold Standard.' I love this hosta: it has withstood the test of time. 'Gold Standard' can seem to be three different plants, depending on the light conditions. In bright light, it will be nearly white with a green edge. In morning sun, it will be bright gold with a green edge, and in deep shade, it will be chartreuse to light green with a darker green edge. The *fortunei* group continues to yield many of the best garden varieties, including 'Antioch' (wide white edge on a green leaf), 'Striptease' (dark green leaf with a wide creamy center), 'Night before Christmas' (large green leaf with a pure white center), and 'Fortunei Aureomarginata' (dark green with a wide gold edge).

I had also become acquainted with the selections and hybrids of *H. sieboldiana*, a species from Japan, but it was not until I began to travel that I realized the true beauty of the plants in this group. It is the gardeners in the cooler climates who do a masterful job with *H. sieboldiana* and also with the closely allied *H.* 'Tokudama' group. *H.* 'Tokudama' produces massive clumps of corrugated blue foliage, and these are the hostas we all dream about in the South. It isn't that we can't grow them: they just don't have quite the triumph they have in the North. Oh, part of it has to do with the fact that the blue on a hosta leaf is wax, and you can guess what happens to wax in 100-degree weather with humidity to match. These hostas just prefer cooler temperatures, like the folks who grow them.

Of course, to the envy of our Northern neighbors, we do a superb job growing the fragrant hostas. The parent of these fragrant blooming hostas was one of only two Chinese species, the heat-loving *H. plantaginea.* It was given the common name of August lily by a prior generation of gardeners, because the clump of shiny green leaves explodes in August with 10-inch-long pure white flowers and an overpowering scent usually encountered only at perfume counters.

It was from this lone species that all the wonderful fragrant hostas that we know today originated. It was New York's Paul Aden who brought the world of fragrant hostas to the forefront with the new varieties he introduced, including 'So Sweet' (round leaves with a wide creamy border and fragrant light lavender flowers), 'Invincible' (thick glossy green leaves and large fragrant purple flowers), and 'Fragrant Bouquet' (smooth golden leaves with a creamy edge and large fragrant flowers). Since these were introduced in the 1980s, the floodgates seem to have burst open.

The real excitement in fragrant flowering hostas came in the mid 1980s, when a double-flowered *H. plantaginea* was imported from China. Folks were gladly shelling out $200 per plant to grow the 10-inch-long fragrant white double flower. The myth outperformed the reality in this case, as the flower would open only if the temperature was just right: not too cool and not too hot. The torture was that buds always formed and swelled, but just before opening . . . poof . . . a stem of limp petal mush.

Then came two variegated-edge plantagineas, 'White Shoulders' (white edge) and 'Heaven Scent' (yellow edge). These highly promoted new hostas with variegation and giant fragrant flowers soon belly-flopped, too. After 'White Shoulders' made it through one winter, it returned as 'No Shoulders.' After that, it wasn't long before this weak grower faded into the sunset. The same was true for 'Heaven Scent,' which was quickly replaced by varieties that actually grew. Only recently has a true variegated *H. plantaginea* entered the market with an edge that actually grows. 'Ming Treasure,' introduced by Mark Zilis of Rochelle, Illinois, promises to be that long-awaited pot of variegation at the end of the rainbow.

The more hybrid hostas I grew, the more I longed to learn about their parent species. All the original hostas are green and will sadly never achieve the popularity of their showier brethren, but each has something to offer. I met *H. venusta* and *H. pulchella*, two of the tiniest hostas, whose mature clumps are only 6 inches wide. *H. nigrescens* is shaped like a wonderful tall vase, as is its offspring, 'Krossa Regal.' *H. yingeri*, discovered on a remote Korean island only in the 1980s, has splendid spider-like flowers that far surpass in elegance any other flowers in the genus hosta. *H. tibae*, with its branched flowerscapes . . . now there is a plant for the breeders.

A virtually unknown group of hostas, one of the most magnificent of the species, grows in cracks on rock cliffs, often near waterfalls. These hostas have large thick leaves, often with white backs for reflecting the sun and heat reflected by the rocks. This group includes *H. hypoleuca, H. rupifraga, H. pycno-phylla*, and *H. longipes*, to name but a few of the species.

Another of the classic hosta species has got to be *H. clausa*. Although it has been in this country for over one hundred years, it is virtually unknown and it is the hosta people most often ask about in our garden. First of all, it runs . . . actually, it gallops in the garden, forming a 10-foot-wide patch in three to four years. Second, the flowers don't open, as indicated by "clausa," which means closed. Each swollen bud has the most incredible colora-tion . . . dark purple, fading to hot pink where the bud attaches to the stem. Imagine what would happen if blue and gold leaf hostas could be bred to cover ground like *H. clausa* . . . oh my my!

It might surprise you to know that well over half the new hostas on the market were discovered as "sports," or mutations on existing cultivars. A hosta is said to sport when its leaf colors mutate into a new pattern. For example, a gold hosta may sport to a gold with a green edge, or any other number of color combinations. The reason that so many sports are found is that hostas are genetically fairly unstable . . . sort of like the folks who collect them. A term has been coined for those who intentionally indulge in the new and wildly popular pastime of searching nurseries for the latest hosta mutations: they are known as "sport fishermen."

In visiting "hosta breeders" around the country, I was shocked to find that the term "breeders" was being used . . . shall I say, quite liberally. Gardeners who find hosta seed growing in their garden consider themselves to be breeders. I think not. In reality, there are only a small handful of people actually making hosta crosses in the entire country.

This is in sharp contrast to the daylily world, where everyone who grows daylilies tries their hand at making crosses. To avoid dealing with 50,000 varieties, many of which are virtually identical, I have strongly promoted my 10-foot rule of breeding. If a new plant cannot be distinguished at 10 feet from a similar-looking plant already recognized in the trade, it should be discarded. Obviously, for this practice to succeed, breeders must be very familiar with existing varieties.

The future of hostas is unlimited. Imagine a plant that was not listed in the top twenty of the perennial popularity poll some short fifteen years ago but has been number one for the last five years. Consider red leaves and red flowers. How about reblooming hostas, how about hostas for hot climates such as those of Texas and Florida . . . How about slug-resistant hostas? Do I think this is an exciting group of plants . . . you bet!

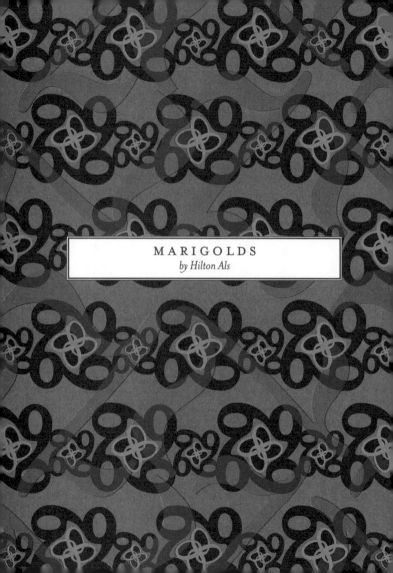

MARIGOLDS
by Hilton Als

I ATE DIRT. I HAD WHAT THEY CALLED the ringworm. I picked my scalp and there it was, underneath my fingernails, piles of sick. I was a pre-teen Caliban deformed by flaky skin; I had pus on my mind. My head was a compost heap. My fingernails dug into what they, the older people, called the ringworm, or eczema, and I sent shivers down my own spine—an erotic "pain" I could not wait to get my hands on. My gray woolen Eton cap was lousy with me. My contemporaries—other children—risked contagion if they touched my cap, let alone my diseased spot, which, come to think of it, looked a little like a woman's private parts; boys spitballed it.

My infirmity sat at the back of my head, just above my neck. My ringworm was my cruddy friend; it had no other friends and so many enzymes, a dark flower could be forced in it. My ringworm was philosophical. It had certain ideas about the world, about me. One thing that made my ringworm sick was my interest in myself—an interest I almost never uttered in the company of the well. My self-interest was not founded on self-love

but on fury over my scabby presence, which no amount of love, from my parents or siblings, could cure. Self-interest ran in my family. They could see me only as the cute extension of what they felt to be cute about themselves. If I expressed, let's say, a dislike of marigolds, that shocked them: I was too cute to contradict flowers. I shut up early on and let my imagination run wild, or as concentrated as my patch of sick.

My ringworm was as infested with longing as I was. My body and soul were a sewer, briny and foul with sexiness. Daddy doesn't like that about me, and I don't like him, but my body craves him.

Daddy says that I am strange, that he never knows what I am talking about. When he comes to call on my mother, he says, Goddamnit-what-the-hell-Jesus-Christ-aw-shit-for-fuck's-sake, and Huh? whenever I open my mouth to speak; consequently, I rarely do. Daddy turns me on because he doesn't think I'm cute; he makes me work for his admiration.

He knows that I spend a lot of my time at the big lending library at Grand Army Plaza in Brook-

lyn, reading books. What he doesn't know is that while there, I also listen to recordings by grand actors reading famous poetry, prose, and plays, as a way of learning how to speak in an authoritative, genteel way meant to captivate my father, like a pus-y siren. I listen to Glenda Jackson as Charlotte Corday in Peter Weiss's play *Marat/Sade*, because she is not genteel or cute in the role of the knife-wielding anarchist: she is a gorgeous hysteric. She contradicts my family for me. One of Charlotte's interlocutors begs her to turn away from her various hatreds and "Look at the trees. Gaze at the rose-colored sky, under which your lovely bosom heaves." Charlotte cannot. "What kind of town is this?" she asks. "I saw peddlers at every corner . . . They're selling little guillotines with sharp knives . . . and dolls filled with red liquid which spurts when the sentence is carried out. What kind of children are these? Who can play with these toys so efficiently? And who is judging? Who is judging?"

As Charlotte Corday, I can hate marigolds. Glenda Jackson's ferocious tone allows me to be the

hysteric I am while imagining Daddy naked, on all fours right behind me, dragging his big Daddy body toward me because I want him to, because I am, finally, all he could ever need: a person capable of screeching, How I hate the marigolds! He bites into my ringworm, and eats the red, pused-out bits in the way my older sister ate the petals she pulled from red flowers: with relish. I am not a child. I am a judge. I have been made older through cultivating need, which feeds my imagination, the one thing Daddy does not have access to, the one thing I can make him a lovesick prisoner of.

I ate dirt because my older sister ate flower petals; Daddy thought my sister's act of floral carnage was charming, just another one of her many idiosyncrasies, like writing poetry, eating chalk, and playing the trumpet. He indulged her because it was safe to: she was a girl. I went her one better by eating dirt from my grandmother's flower bed. For a time, dirt was the sustenance I relied on in order to gain strength and wreak the revenge I wanted

against all the time my father did not love or pay attention to my sore spot.

The soily pebbles in my mouth, which I ingested in clumps, came from the wormy ground my grandmother cultivated in the yard behind her house in Brooklyn. The house was large, dark, and old. The worms in her yard were not as dark as my ringworm, despite the dirt they clung to. My grandmother, Frances, rushed about in her garden, planning, picking, and planting. She'd drop slowly to her knees in a little bed of marigolds. She ran her fingers through their hard heads, just as she ran her fingers through my sick head from time to time, unmindful of illness.

I can see those marigolds now, bad-tempered and alive, carrot-colored and stiff, like my grandmother, who was considered a parody of a Jew among black Americans who worked for her, from time to time, as day laborers. She was a West Indian woman with blue-gray eyes set in a long face, who had an interest in thrift, fortitude, and acquiring real estate. She had three children, two of whom

lived with her and her husband, my grandfather, a man she had made a stranger to her body long before I came along. My father lived on the top floor of her old, dark house; he would not leave his mother, no matter how many children he had with my mother, who, when she bathed me, called my private parts posies. My mother, young and ill; my father will never marry anything not well, not his mother.

In my grandmother's garden, Daddy uproots the black earth. He cuts things down and picks tomatoes, too. And in the green dusk he eats some of the vegetables he has picked. Sitting in a metal chair painted white, wearing a white T-shirt with thin straps, he drinks Scotch and perspires. His fat Daddy breasts, bigger than any mother's, flop on either side of his thin T-shirt straps. I can see his nipples, dark against his iodine-brown skin. It is late summer, the summer of my scratching. That was the summer I was sent to stay with my grandmother and her children because my mother was ill. My mother had been sent away to the land of the sick, which I imagine—when I am not imagining as

much of Daddy as I can stand—to be a land filled with flowers, flowers as fulfilling to the eyes of the sick as I am filled with longing for flowers to sprout from my own little patch of fertile ground, my ringworm.

Standing before Daddy, long after Grandmother has gone indoors, finds me standing in rank earth with blood on my hands, scratching as I compete with marigolds for his attention. He is crouched in the part of the garden devoted to marigolds as I imagine lifting my patch of ringworm, like a veil. I am his bride, my arms heavy with bouquets of good health and well-being.

OVID AT TOMI
by Dan Chiasson

for my mother's marigolds

I
HIS BED

At Tomi, Ovid's tenancy—

Estrangement—

No consolation, writing
nagging letters home.

No creature there could fill itself with air

like the speckled, rare

Italian salamander.

2
HIS DESK

This insulating care takes
everyone.

This gauze

(Though thick, layer upon layer
Smothering the patient),

This white. Fine, like dust,
but uninspectable. His
window opens to an elm's great
heaviness, now sagging

with March
snow: hardened,
making wide, exaggerated boughs,
obscuring threads of boughs,
boughlets born last August.

Lost.

When Ovid was at Rome,
the favorite of Germanicus,

whose derelict smile Rome watched,

pointing—

Imagine Rome a dream even for the Roman.

3
HIS MIRROR

He dreamed he was the spade
his mother used

to dig her marigolds in spring,
her *bloom* and *worry.*

Her plunging, throwing, patting
to bring rows to life,
each bloom familiar

to worry, every row perfect, bloom,

rich dirt between, planned
absence and full, superfluous bloom—

He made the trench her hand proposed.

He was the pressure in her palm.

Her *ache from planting*

was

his *presence in her life.*

4
HIS WALK

That it should
Bother him,

After the indignity
Of dressing without

Light; the heavy
Trudging; pack's

Weight; necessity
Of bundling; that

The scraping of
One leaf, drawn

Across the snow's
March, hardened skin

Then withdrawn, upright
Animate on its stem,

Billowed into flight,
Fallen, that one leaf

Bringing Rome to mind
Should bother him—

That thrushes fatten there
for supper.

5
HIS MIRROR

Then he dreamed he chose
The purple blouse his mother

Wore the morning she conceived
Him—dressed her, felt her

Expectation as his own, her life
Now distillate of her only wish,

Her saying yes to the thing
Thrown over her.

6
HIS DESK

Industrious mornings
Left this long, white

Afternoon to count
The absences, then night.

Work was no consolation.
Ask the praegustator

About work, its joys,
Its privilege. In Rome,

A girl's bright misled
Questions ferried him

To rest. Here no one
Speaks in sentences.

Life, even this room,
Especially this room,

His photographs, his
Desk, mirror, bed

Shrivel like old pears.
Once in Rome a pomegranate's

Juices stained
His whole face purple.

There isn't an imagination,
Only the mind's tired

Circling for truth. No one
Invented the poinsettia.

Its red leaves open
Now, the windowpane.

7

HIS BED

(after *Tristia*, Book IV)

It is sure misfortune
for a child to marry.

God's will is otherwise,
and so the girl I called

sweet names died while still
indistinct to me. Picturing

her now is like picturing the moon
close up, the chalky surface of the moon.

The next was blameless, pretty
enough, no prize. Once

I surprised her kneading dough
for that night's bread and she

was anxious afterwards
for hours. Now

my love, my third, best wife
sobs constantly for me.

She counts my absence on
a calendar. Why do I

imagine her betraying me?

    —At dawn, after an all-
    night party, as she lies on

a banquet table strewn
with half-eaten plums,

upended drinking cups,
wine running from the table

in a narrow ribbon, hair
back, begging for the cocks

of twenty lined-up drunkards—

Thank God my mother died

before she saw
her boy brought here

by boat, dropped here
beside the Danube.

THIRTEEN ROSES
by David Raffeld

I
Mother, although these are red of blood
the green thumb of death grew them.

II
Yes, it's their smell
that's keeping you alive.

III
These are not roses a lover brings.
They ask for nothing given
in return.

IV
Go, my mother, get ready for your journey.
How far? Only the roses
beside your bed know.

V
Who will dry these,
press them into the page labeled
last date or life jilted at the altar?

VI
Mother, even the word prose
has a rose in it.
Had these words a nose
they'd smell your death
turning into poetry.

VII
A mile from the ocean
doesn't explain the bead of salt
on the lip of every rose.

VIII
Mother, the roses are drinking up
your dying smell, tripping up death!
Come on, for just a few hours
you can open your eyes!

IX
Beyond, or beneath language
your breathing is invisible.
Though the roses are living off your death
they won't toll their red bells—
they'd be working on the Sabbath.

X
Mother, they're going
too heavy in their heads now,
too delicate in their stems.
Soon they will shatter
into green bloody glass.

XI

A thorn pricks death &
it loses just a drop
of black plasma.

XII

Mother, when you die
one fat worm will crawl
out from each rose.

XIII

When you depart your body
will open your spirit
will cross over these twelve roses
of the Red Sea into Jerusalem.

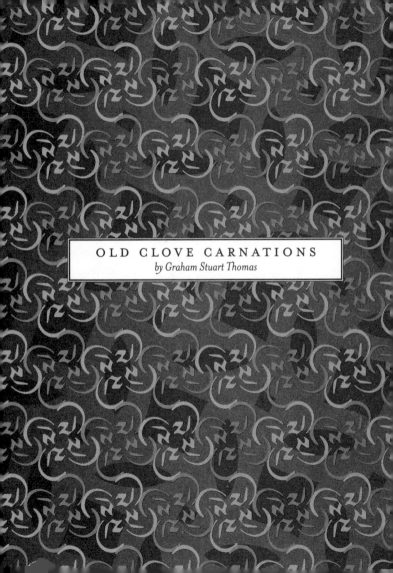

OLD CLOVE CARNATIONS
by Graham Stuart Thomas

THE HISTORY OF THE CARNATION is closely entwined with that of the pink. Identical in name—"pink" and "carnation" actually mean the same thing—but only fraternally related, they are both favorites of mine, but the carnation, and particularly the old clove carnation, has always reigned supreme in my affections. The flowers and the foliage of carnations are larger than those of pinks, which are descended from several species smaller than *Dianthus caryophyllus*, the wild type of carnation. The wild carnation is found in poor limy soils in central and southern Europe and may frequently be seen growing in the mortar of old buildings. Both pinks and carnations have long been favourites with the English-speaking nations, and as with so many other flowers, it was their fragrance which brought them popularity. Those with the richest scent, similar to that of cloves, are my special delight, and indeed it is a rich and uncommon fragrance, scarcely found in other flowers.

As long ago as 1629, John Parkinson sought to call our attention to the beauties of carnations by

describing those that he knew in his great book *Paradisi in Sole, Paradisus terrestris*, which was really a pun on his own name. He recorded only a few doubles of the species, which have been lost to us long since. Numerous varieties became very popular during the eighteenth century but suffered a setback when carpet bedding became the vogue in the nineteenth century. A new impetus was provided by the variety 'Mrs. T. W. Lawson,' which was raised at Ellis in Massachusetts in 1895: it was the first repeat-flowering kind, and thereafter such varieties became popular at the expense of the once-flowering old ones.

The old carnations have a special point in their favour and that is that they flower in the month of August, well after all the old garden pinks are finished. It has been my good fortune to rediscover one variety, the famous Old Salmon Clove. Its real name is Lord Chatham, and the earliest reference to it that I have found is 1780. It is so recorded in *Old Carnations and Pinks* (1955) by C. Oscar Moreton. (Mr. Moreton did so much to awaken interest in these plants that it is a matter of great sadness that

other growers did not carry on his good work.) The
Earl of Chatham, the source of the name Lord
Chatham, was of course the famous William Pitt,
Prime Minister, who died in 1788. During its long
life 'Lord Chatham' has been inexplicably known as
'Raby Castle,' after a noted dwelling in the north of
England. Indeed, most of the old carnations I have
found have been growing in gardens in the north
and west of the British Isles. 'Lord Chatham' is a
good grower with splendid, broad, blue-grey foliage; its stems reach some 18 inches but need support. The colour of the flower is near to that of
uncooked salmon, not the usual salmon pink. It
can be readily propagated by cuttings or by layers.
These are points in its favour, but its clove scent is
the real delight. In old books I have not found any
reference to this variety producing sports with
flowers of different colour or form, and thus it was
with great pleasure I came across one, with flowers
of salmon red flaked with white. (The word "flake"
is a term always used by old writers when describing
flowers in which the colours are striped.) This variant was found by Mrs. Phyllis Marshall in a garden

at Donghadee, in Northern Ireland, some twenty years ago. Her husband is head gardener at the noted garden of Mount Stewart in that same province. Named 'Phyllis Marshall,' the variant reverted once to the normal colour of 'Lord Chatham,' thus proving its identity.

Other variants I have found have no name, but among them is the flower always called, rightly or wrongly, the 'Old Crimson Clove.' This one I have known all my life: it was a favourite for my father's daily buttonhole. These flowers have remarkable rejuvenating powers: after being worn all day their stalks may be cut and again split and, after a night in water, will serve for another day. The 'Old Crimson' is, as its name suggests, a very dark red with its own strong perfume and good foliage.

What these old plants do not enjoy is an enclosed garden on acid soil. They then need frequent propagation. Lime seems to be an essential. Cuttings are best torn off the stem with a heel and inserted into sandy soil in early September. They should root and be ready for planting in their appointed positions in spring. Layers are made by

acutely bending a branch or shoot of a plant (splitting the joint with a knife at the stem is sometimes an aid) and burying the free end of the shoot in sandy soil while the other end is still attached to the parent plant, keeping the new shoot firm by means of a peg or, better, a stone or half brick. The old plants set no seeds.

Members of the genus *Dianthus*, including both the carnation and the pink, have also sometimes been called the "gillyflower." The term is also attached to wallflowers (*Cheiranthus*). The name has a long and interesting history. Put briefly, the plant from which cloves are obtained is *Caryophyllon*; the buds of a pink resemble somewhat the buds of a clove (it is in the bud stage that the cloves of commerce are harvested), and the fragrance of pinks and carnations certainly resembles that of cloves. Further, the leaves of *Caryophyllon* (nut-leafed), an Indian spice, are supposed to resemble the leaves of a walnut. Thus, the name of a spice-bearing plant with leaves resembling those of a walnut—the nut of Jupiter—became transferred to the flower of Jupiter—Dianthus—and thus to the family *Caryophyl-*

laceae, and *Dianthus caryophyllus*. Gillyflower is a corruption of *caryophyllus* and is spelt variously: as giroflée (French), garafalo (Italian), gilloflower (English). Forty-four years before the printing of the Authorised Version of the Bible, Barnaby Googe wrote: "O what sweete and goodly Gely floures are here, you may truely say that Solomon in all his princely pompe was never able to attayne to this beauty."

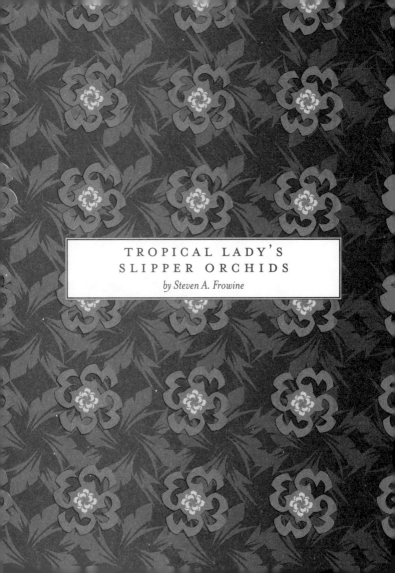

TROPICAL LADY'S
SLIPPER ORCHIDS

by Steven A. Frowine

I LOVE THE TROPICS. IT'S A BALMY PART of the world where all life seems mellower and more exuberant and plants and creatures of all types show off their dazzling and outlandish color combinations. Maybe this is the way they express their appreciation for being born in such a heady place, where formality and rigid ideas about "proper" color schemes and design are blown away by the warm, humid trade winds and replaced with a freer, uninhibited, anything-goes kind of attitude.

By growing orchids, plants that exemplify the tropics, I am able to enjoy the exotic at home all year round, even through the snowy New England winter. Orchids represent one of the largest of all plant families, and their diversity of complex flower forms is immense and very different from that of most temperate plants. Of all the wonderful orchids in the world, the lady's slipper is my favorite.

The lady's slipper orchid is named for its central petal or "lip," which is shaped much like a slipper: from a botanical point of view, this is what distinguishes it from myriad other orchids. Some of my friends find these slipper-shaped flowers with petals sporting hairs and bumps strange or unappealing, but to me their otherworldliness is alluring. The waxy blossoms, in a wide range of unlikely color combinations of greens, reds, pinks, whites, and burgundies, are borne on fuzzy, pipe cleaner–like stems. Once the flowers open, they put on a show for four to six weeks, sometimes longer; many varieties will bloom more than once a year.

I'm attracted to the foliage of the lady's slipper almost as much as to the flowers. Unlike the downright homely leaves of many other orchids, the leaves of the lady's slipper are strikingly beautiful, either a rich, glossy green or variegated, in mosaic patterns of dark and emerald green. This ornamental foliage is a highly desirable feature, since all orchids bloom for a relatively brief time each year.

Within the lady's slipper group, I have lots of favorites. I really enjoy the petite white species and their hybrids. *Paphiopedilum niveum* is a dainty gem with pristine white flowers borne above dark-green, marbled foliage; *Paphiopedilum bellatulum* is a charming horticultural treasure with larger flowers than *P. niveum* and burgundy spots. Most common white hybrids have one or both of these parent species in their background.

The Chinese species of lady's slippers are also quite intriguing, and of special interest to me since my wife is from Beijing. Unlike many of the *Paphiopedilum* species discovered long ago in the mid-1800s, the Chinese species were only recently brought to the attention of orchid aficionados, in the 1980s. These lady's slippers are decidedly different from other Paphiopedilums and look strikingly similar to the terrestrial cypripediums, our native lady's slippers. Their lips are pronounced and look more like pouches or purses than slippers. *Paphiopedilum armeniacum* and *Paphiopedilum micranthum* are particularly striking. The flowers of both are disproportionately huge. *P. armeniacum* has a sunny, golden-yellow flower while *P. micranthum* displays a rosy pink pouch with lighter pink surrounding petals. The strong pink and clear yellow of these recently discovered lady's slippers make orchid hybridizers dream of until-now-unheard-of cross-breeding possibilities. Another fabulous Asian newcomer, this time from Vietnam, is called *Paphiopedilum delenatii*. This delicate pink-flowering species has a light fragrance, a rare and enviable trait for a lady's slipper orchid.

Like all orchids, lady's slippers grow literally forever. If you give these plants a modest amount of care they will reward you with perpetual life. Each year they continue to produce divisions, growing larger and more spectacular every time. "Paphs," as they are nicknamed, attain full glory when they reach a specimen size of ten or more growths. Every time one of my larger plants is in full bloom, it is a guaranteed showstopper.

When the plant gets too large for its pot, the perfect opportunity presents itself for enjoying one of life's finest pleasures: sharing a piece of treasure with a plant-crazed friend. I was on the receiving end of this equation about twenty-five years ago when I was given a division of a very fine and cherished plant, with a distinguished name to match. This lady's slipper orchid was the *Paphiopedilum* Maudiae Claire de Lune 'Edgard Van Belle' and was a present from a dear older friend and a fine gentle-man in Cleveland. He has been a friend for many years, and though we are separated by distance, every time this spectacular plant with exquisite fo-liage and elegant green and white flowers puts on its display, I think of him fondly. 'Edgard Van Belle' has grown large enough now that I am able to share divisions of it with my good friends, who I hope will, in turn, think of me when their plant blooms. A rewarding cycle!

Some particularly magnificent lady's slippers have multiple regal blossoms. The most spectacular and majestic is *Paphiopedilum rothschildianum*. This species is thought to be endemic to Mount Kina-balu in Borneo, an appropriately mysterious hab-itat for such a rare orchid. Its huge blossoms, of which there are usually two to four per 22-inch flower stalk, can measure up to 15 inches in diame-ter. The plant itself is no less imposing, with leaves up to 30 inches long. I have seen it in bloom in a greenhouse, and its display is breathtaking, but it is so immense that I don't have space for it in my light garden. *Paphiopedilum philippinense*, a smaller, albeit

still stunning relative of the giant, has bloomed for me a few times. It has multiple, brightly marked flowers with long, pendulous, twisted petals.

North American lady's slipper orchids are now easier for gardeners to acquire. In past years, they were unscrupulously dug from the wild and sold to unsuspecting gardeners, but now they are grown from seed and the right species do not require extraordinary gardening skill. The yellow lady's slipper orchids, *Cypripedium parviflorum* and *C. parviflorum* var. *pubescens*, are both easy to grow and are a unique addition to any partially shaded garden with moist soil. With the development of new lab-growing techniques, many more species will soon be available.

Rarely is it true in life that things of value come easily; lady's slippers are the exception. Except for the rare forms, they are not expensive, and they are easy to grow. I grow all my tropical species in the basement under tiered, four-tube fluorescent light carts. This method of growing suits the mobile life my horticultural career causes me to lead. The plants are potted in small, 3- to 6-inch plastic pots

in a mixture of fir bark and charcoal. This is not a secret formula and many different recipes work equally well. Lady's slippers merely require a mix that drains well but also retains some moisture. Since I use bark, which tends to be a nitrogen hog, I fertilize with a slow-release fertilizer high in nitrogen, like Osmocote or a water-soluble fertilizer formulated for orchids. I repot my orchids every year in the spring when I move them outside to the lathe house, which provides about 50 percent shade. I keep all my plants in this summer retreat from about early June until September, when the evenings begin to get cool, but move them before the first frost. The cool evenings help the flower buds set for winter blooms: the plants must experience about a 15° temperature difference between day and night.

Lady's slippers will tell you if they are being grown well. Their foliage should be dark green and healthy. If your plants are not flowering, either they are not receiving enough light or they are not getting the 15° day/night temperature differential. Fortunately, they are bothered by very few insect

pests or diseases. They are sometimes attacked by a bit of scale or mealy bugs, either of which can be controlled with superior horticultural oils, Neem, or insecticidal soaps. Leaf spots, leaf tip dieback, or crown rot occasionally causes problems, but can be stopped with a good greenhouse disinfectant like Physan 20 or RD 20.

I can't really imagine my life without lady's slipper orchids. I've been growing them since high school and they have traveled with me everywhere I moved. They never fail to excite me with their dependable, exotic blooms. If you would like a touch of the tropics at home, then lady's slipper orchids are definitely for you. They are fun and rewarding to grow and, with so many different species and hybrids, will provide you, as they have me, with a lifetime of possibilities and pleasure.

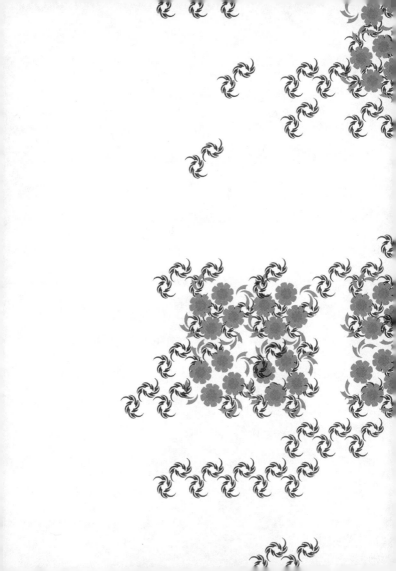

HONEYPOTS AND
SILVER TREE

by Ernest Wilson

A S A MATTER OF FACT, APART FROM the very cold regions of the globe, every country can boast of a general miscellany of trees, shrubs, and herbs noteworthy for the beauty of their flowers. The Cape, we have already shown, is no exception and in addition possesses four well-marked types each of sufficient merit to make the country remarkable. These four types—succulent plants, bulbous plants, proteas and heaths—dominate the floral features of the Cape of Good Hope. Heaths, bulbous and succulent plants are found in other parts of the world, though in less variety, but the glorious proteas are peculiarly South African. Brilliant inflorescences are characteristic of the Cape flora, and in this respect the only region in the world with which fair comparisons can be made is western Australia. In both lands Proteaceae, a family of endless variety of forms, is a striking floristic feature. What the genus *Banksia* is to Western Australia, protea is to South Africa; yet this genus is even less known in American gardens than is *Banksia*. Proteas are common in the immediate vicinity of Cape Town as well as throughout the whole of the coastal plateau; a few species are found in the more elevated and drier regions to the north. Some, like *Protea grandiflora*, are trees of moderate size, others, like *Protea amplexicaulis* and *Protea cordata*, almost hug the ground, but the vast majority are bushes from 6 to 10 feet tall, with erect stems and huge, terminal, handsome heads of flowers. Such heads consist of very many elongated, relatively simple flowers having no petals but with colored calyx and bracts enclosed and nestling within seried rows of tall colored scaly, more or less erect, floral bracts—nests of colored, fluffy down guarded by projecting stamens and pistils suggesting the quills of a fledgling bird-of-paradise. The first species to be figured in European literature was *Protea neriifolia* by Clusius in his *Exoticarum* (p. 38, fig. 15) published in 1605, as "Cardui generis elegantissimi, etc." The specimen is said to have come from Madagascar, but much more probably it came from the shores of Algoa Bay or those of Table Bay. This species is widespread and its large flower heads with velvety black apical tufts of hairs bearding the upright involucral scales are strikingly handsome. Nowadays about one hundred species are known, and all are worth a place in the best Californian gardens, yet Bailey's *Cyclopedia* mentions three only (*Protea cynaroides, Protea mellifera,* and *Protea nana*) in cultivation in this country. Overflowing with honey are the pink and white heads of *Protea mellifera*, known to the Boers as "honeypots." The honey is collected and made into a kind of sugar, the blossoming season being a great occasion for picnics. Striking is the inflorescence of *Protea speciosa*, with tufts of black hairs on the tips of the inner involucral bracts; but none are finer than the glossy-leafed *P. cynaroides*, common and widespread from Cape Town to Grahamstown in the east. The involucral bracts of this species vary from nearly white to silvery rose; the heads are from 10 to 12 inches across and the plants from 1 to 10 feet tall. It favors rocky places, and to come suddenly upon this plant in blossom, to look down into its wondrous beauty as it nestles amid rocks, is a delight never to be forgotten. It has been my good fortune to see either under cultivation or under their natural conditions nearly all the known flowers of exceptional merit. I have a generous meed of praise for each and every one but, in my judgment, the handsomest inflorescence in the world is that of *P. cynaroides* seen on its native heath.

WISTERIA
by Philip Levine

The first purple wisteria
I recall from boyhood hung
on a wire outside the windows
of the breakfast room next door
at the home of Steve Pisaris.
I loved his tall, skinny daughter,
or so I thought, and I would wait
beside the back door, prostrate,
begging to be taken in. Perhaps
it was only the flowers of spring
with their sickening perfumes
that had infected me. When Steve
and Sophie and the three children
packed up and made the move west,
I went on spring after spring,
leaden with desire, half-asleep,
praying to die. Now I know
those prayers were answered.
That boy died, the brick houses
deepened and darkened with rain,
age, use, and finally closed
their eyes and dreamed the sleep

of California. I learned this
only today. Wakened early
in an empty house not lately
battered by storms, I looked
for nothing. On the surface
of the rain barrel, the paled,
shredded blossoms floated.

DELPHINIUMS
by Thomas Fischer

I PUT IT ALL DOWN TO MR. LEWIS. HE was a kindly old gentleman with a neat silver mustache who lived next door to the cottage my family rented one summer in Melvin Village, New Hampshire. Besides his mustache, he had two outstanding qualities: he was remarkably tolerant of inquisitive little boys (it probably helped that I liked flowers) and he raised delphiniums, what seemed like hundreds of them, massed in one big bed. My seven-year-old eyes had never seen such glory. More than all the other natural wonders of the place—the bluebirds and grosbeaks, the lake, the Old Man of the Mountain—those six-foot spires of brilliant ultramarine held me transfixed. I was imprinted, like one of Konrad Lorenz's goslings, and ever since, I've been trotting along after that remembered image of perfect blueness, trying to catch up.

It hasn't been easy. In southern New England, where I garden, delphiniums shouldn't be among the Impossible Blue Flowers—plants like alpine gentians or nivalid primulas (both of which I have tried to grow and have been justly punished for my

hubris). And yet my early attempts with them were disastrous. The Pacific Giants, which are the only delphiniums widely available in the United States, behaved like spoiled, sickly aristocrats. They sulked. They mildewed. They demanded to be trussed up. They languished in the July heat. When they died, usually after only a single season, I was secretly glad.

At first I thought my slovenly gardening skills were to blame. But then an afternoon spent with some old issues of the bulletin of the American Delphinium Society turned up some interesting facts. As many delphinium fanciers know, the Pacific Giants were developed by Frank Reinelt, a Czech gardener who emigrated to the United States in 1925 and soon thereafter helped found the firm of Vetterle & Reinelt in Capitola, California. What is not so well known is that Reinelt used the short-lived, red-flowered American species *Delphinium cardinale* in his breeding program, both to produce pink-flowered hybrids and to intensify the color of his blues, which he found "rather cold" without the *D. cardinale* genetic admixture but "brilliant, alive, and warm" with it. The fact that his Pacific Giants

also tended to behave like annuals bothered him not at all. In 1944 he wrote: "Here [in the U.S.] . . . hardly any plant lives longer than two years . . . True perennialism is not as important a factor as the color, size of flower, size of spike and habit." The legacy of this rather airy dismissal has been generations of frustrated, delphinium-phobic gardeners.

Even though it was comforting to be able to ascribe my failure to a lousy gene pool, it still didn't help in my search for a growable delphinium. I was just about ready to resign myself to a diminished, delphinium-less existence when I discovered the writings, and later the delphiniums, of the great German gardener Karl Foerster (coincidentally, another kindly old gentleman with a silver mustache). Between 1911 and his death in 1970 at the age of ninety-six, Foerster selected and named more than six hundred perennial cultivars at his nursery in Bornim, outside Berlin. (You can still find some of Foerster's asters, heleniums, phloxes, and salvias at almost any good perennial nursery.) Of the many books Foerster wrote, the one I most

wanted to read was *Blauer Schatz der Gärten* (*Blue Garden Treasure*), which has two whole chapters on delphiniums, but with my wobbly college German it proved quite a challenge. Foerster writes in a dense, quasi-mystical style that might best be characterized as High Rhapsodic; his introduction to the book, "Blue in the World and in the Garden," is an almost religious invocation of the color blue as an all-pervading cosmic energy. Elsewhere, he claims that blueness is the equivalent in color of the chorus's startling modulation on the words *vor Gott* in the last movement of Beethoven's Ninth Symphony. This was schnapps straight from the bottle. Still, it was worth the effort to persevere, for I learned that, in his breeding work with delphiniums, beauty was only one of Foerster's goals—equally important were vigor, disease resistance, strong, upright flower stalks, and true perenniality. The illustrations of the plants that embodied these desirable traits sent me into covetous fits. I was pining to fill my garden with 'Fernzünder' and 'Tempelgong' and 'Perlmutterbaum,' but where could I find them? Not, as a search of the cata-

logues revealed, at any of the U.S. nurseries that routinely ſtocked Foerſter's other plants; in fact, not at any American nursery at all—a ſtate of affairs that ſtrikes me as one of the great horticultural myſteries of our time.

It wasn't until I made a trîp to Germany in the fall of 1993 that I finally found the mother lode of Foerſter delphiniums. I had been curious about German nurseries for some time, and one that came highly recommended was the Staudengärtnerei Klose, near the cîty of Kassel. Here, along wîth thousands of other tempting perennials, the Klose family has assembled *fifty-two* named delphinium cultivars, more than half of them Foerſter's. Exercising superhuman self-reſtraint, I bought only two, mindful that, in order to get them home legally, I would have to wash all the soil from their roots back at my hotel (hotel managers hate ît when you do that; ît's something about the pîpes) and present them to the USDA for inſpection. The plants I chose were two that Foerſter himself considered among his beſt: 'Berghimmel,' sky blue wîth a whîte "eye"—the contraſting center of the

269

flower—and, for balance, 'Finſteraarhorn,' deep
gentian blue with a black eye.

Back home, I began to worry. After their trau-
matic journey, the plants looked squashed and not
at all as though they were looking forward to life in
a new land. I potted them up and waited. Almoſt
immediately, cheerful tufts of new foliage appeared
and grew so vigorously that I decided to risk planting them out in the garden, even though ît was now
mid-Oĉtober. They seemed not to mind. By April,
each had formed a dome of fresh, pale green
growth; by May, flower ſtalks appeared; finally, in
late June, the buds opened: pure, ravishing,
longed-for blueness. Delphiniums that Karl
Foerſter had named over sixty years ago were
blooming in my garden. After the flowers had gone
by, I cut them back, happy to waît a year for their
reappearance. As ît turned out, I had to waît only a
few weeks: they bloomed again, and again, and
again.

That did ît. Two delphiniums were not
enough. I diſpatched a letter to the Staudengärtnerei Klose. Would they consider shîpping plants

to the United States, providing one had the proper permit? Yes, they would. Off went an order for twenty-eight delphiniums, plus a few other odds and ends. (You have to grow *something* with your delphiniums.) Though they were in transit for more than three weeks, they had been beautifully packed, and most survived and eventually prospered. Now, from mid-June until fall, the garden is almost never without the ghostly near-white of 'Gletscherwasser,' the dark velvet of 'Tropennacht,' the mountain-lake sapphire of 'Jubelruf.' I even like their mouth-filling Teutonic names, with their associations of sky and water and precious minerals.

In his book *Garten als Zauberschlüssel* (*The Garden as a Magic Key*), Foerster wrote: "In every zone of the world and every month of the year, somewhere or other the blue fire is blooming forth." If he's watching, up there in some delphinium-blue gardener's Valhalla, I hope he knows I'm keeping the flame burning.

A FAVORITE PLANT
by Geoffrey B. Charlesworth

HOW TO CHOOSE A FAVORITE PLANT? "Favorite" is not a fixed attribute, and with plants it is especially susceptible to change with the seasons. Is it possible to say your favorite plant is a snowdrop in the abundance of May?

Perhaps it would be helpful to list the qualities I admire most in a plant and try to reach "favorite" by consensus—that is, consensus of the several competing and conflicting emotions that plants evoke. To begin with, I must favor the plants I have raised from seed. Propagation from seed has been my obsession for the last twenty-five years or more, and there is immense satisfaction to be obtained from this close involvement with a plant. So I have to rule out those many beautifully named daylilies, irises, and peonies that crowd the catalogues, virtually all trees and shrubs, all the bulbs of Holland, the gorgeous double-flowered clones of bloodroot, trillium, and anemonella, the color forms of hepatica and *Anemone nemorosa*, the fanciful forms of *Primula sieboldii* and the show auriculas and the lovely color forms of mountain and moorland plants discovered by a lucky hiker or a diligent searcher. Many white forms of campanula, gold-and-silver-leafed heathers, red-streaked and blotched heucheras and tiarellas, and hundreds of hybrid porophylla saxifrages must be excluded, too.

The next consideration is size. I grow many kinds of plants—far too many—but I primarily think of myself as a "rock gardener"—someone who grows "alpine plants," though these pigeonholing terms are very flexible and everybody who tries to define exactly what it is they are doing or what group of plants they are talking about runs into consistency trouble. Anyway, because true alpine plants are never annual, I shall have to eliminate the wonderful annuals from the Southern hemisphere, from Texas and the hot deserts of the Southwest, the meadow plants from the prairies and the woodlanders from the Appalachians.

I grow (i.e., sow the seed of) every draba and androsace I can find. Typical would be *Draba rigida*, whose tiny leaves crowd together into a rock-hard, tight, compact, gray-green mound. This surely suggests an infatuation with if not a profound admiration and love for such bun-shaped plants: those inhabitants of the wild cliffs, screes, and rocky tundra of all alpine regions of the world. Many dianthus species start life as buns, but after two or three seasons become exuberant cushions or mats and lose some of their charm in the process. Some summer and fall gentians promise bun status in early spring, but spread out their leafy tentacles as the year progresses, unceremoniously swamping their near neighbors. A dense texture is almost a necessity in deciding on a favorite plant.

Color is also very important. For some gardeners, whose main aim is to form "color schemes" of blue and white or orange and magenta, it is paramount. Since the color-specific garden is such a chancy proposition, these gardeners might settle for color "associations" of two or, with luck, three plants. The results might last long enough for the gardener to take a roll of film as proof that the scheme works. It is very difficult for rock gardeners to choose neighbors by color alone and almost impossible to use color for large-scale effect. Though the rock gardener's May-June extravaganza features every color nature has to offer, it would be idle to distort her bountiful mélange by selecting or deselecting particular plants for the color of their flowers. This is not to imply that rock gardeners are indifferent to the charm of flower color, but leaf color and texture are valued most, since rock plants usually stand in isolation and must decorate the garden for the whole growing season, and in some cases for the winter, too. The hair and bristles on leaf and stem, whose function is to soak up powerful sunlight and to protect plants from excesses of temperature change and moisture, give many plants their gray or white leaf color. In some plants temperature changes create attractive reds and purples. The exquisite leaf colors of the eriogonums of the U.S. West are an example of that kind of evolution.

My list of desirable traits seems to be leading me straight to *Draba rosularis*, a soft gray bun from Turkey. But we like people not just because they are good, kind, and pretty but for some indefinable spark, usually called "chemistry," that draws us to them and begs not to be analyzed too closely. Just so with plants. In that case, my favorite has to be *Physo-*

plexis comosa. This is not merely because I am writing at the beginning of July, when the plant approaches maximum attractiveness.

Physoplexis is a genus with only one species. It was separated recently from phyteuma, which itself is not a very prepossessing group of plants. The common name of phyteuma is rampion; rampion is also a common name for the edible root of *Campanula rapunculoides*. In phyteuma, the dowdy cousin of campanula, the bells of campanula are reduced to narrow tubes collected into a spherical (or prolate ellipsoidal) head. The flowers are mostly a dingy purple, but some are a nice clear blue. The plants don't usually make mats but spread by seed, sometimes taking over the garden like some of their obstreperous campanula relatives.

In physoplexis the narrow tubes of phyteuma are replaced by an intriguing bottle-shaped corolla, a flask with a rounded bottom and a long, thin "neck," with the style sticking out of the bottle's virtually closed mouth and appearing to extend the neck (it is because the "petals" are fused together that physoplexis has been separated from phyteuma). The color is a soft pearly mauve, while the tip of the neck and the style are deep purple. The bottles are all joined at their bases (actually there are tiny stalks, but these are not visible) to form a bunch of bottles. The umbels, for that is what they are, are at the end of 3-inch stems and surrounded by a circle of leaves. The effect is rather like onions with dried stalks intact sitting on a plate of leaves. The plant is "difficult" for no obvious single reason. It is rare in nature, found only in the rocky limestone regions of south Europe: the Dolomites of Italy and the Julian Alps of Slovenia (but lime is not essential to grow it). Gardeners on holiday are not able to obtain much seed in the wild, and it doesn't always appear on seedlists, though there are a few Czech collectors who have it on their own specialist lists. Seed often takes two years to germinate, but the process can be accelerated using gibberellic acid. Then the seedlings grow so slowly that you can transplant to individual pots only in the second season after germination, and it is only in late summer that the plants are ready to be planted outside. Anything this slow has a long period of

vulnerability and is more subject to accident than
to horticultural mismanagement. Gardeners all
over the world denounce slugs as major hazards.
Slugs distinguish physoplexis seedlings from thousands of their neighbors and unerringly destroy
overnight what took three years to achieve. Many
campanulas are similarly cursed, and usually only
the least desirable species are exempt. But gardeners do not dwell too long on catastrophe. Failure is
an accepted part of daily life and we value our successes the more.

Physoplexis gives us more pleasurable anticipation than most plants. It is deciduous, so you
begin the spring not knowing whether it has survived the winter. When the shoots finally appear, it
is quite late and there is a surge of joy and pride.
The leaves, almost purple at first, are a dark glossy
green, like English holly, but more circular and
without prickles. Physoplexis doesn't form a bun,
alas! You would have to call it a clump, almost a
loose clump. The leaves are not tiny and tight, nor
are they gray. But the total effect is better than the
sum of its parts: the rounded clump is no bigger

than the exquisitely compact draba even after four or five years, and the end result is a globular plant. If you walked through my garden at moderate speed, you might not see it, even in the standard rock-gardener posture, with head bent and eyes firmly fixed on the ground; it is not flamboyant in the least. Only if you are familiar with its quaint beauty or if it is pointed out to you by a happy gardener could you expect to notice it.

Physoplexis must be given some shade in New England to prevent its shriveling up. A plant in too much sun may retire belowground early and wait until the following spring to reappear. Yet it is not in a woodland garden or in any situation where there is any competition. A raised bed, a crevice garden, or a container would be the natural place to plant it. There is no advantage to keeping it in a greenhouse, since it is perfectly hardy in the Northeast. I have five or six plants at the moment: one in a crevice, two in a container that used to be a hollow log found by the roadside, a couple in raised beds. There are also a few still too young to plant out. I constantly forget where they all are, even though I look at them nearly every day. I have considered marking their positions with red plastic labels so that I can find them without crawling around on my knees. Kneeling or squatting is required for looking at a plant properly in any case, but since I can no longer manage either posture for very long at a time I may be reduced to taking pictures with a telephoto lens. A bed raised to chest level would be ideal for viewing, but it is now too late in my life for me to think of such major additions to the garden, even for physoplexis.

I hope my passion for *Physoplexis comosa* is not seen merely as elitist, though it is certainly that. Nor obscure, though many gardeners have never grown it. There are many, many beautiful plants from the mountains and tundras of the world, enough to satisfy any gardener's desire for novelty. No one has seen everything, and it takes the same kind of judgment and experience to recognize the beauty of rock plants as it takes to recognize any work of art.

PRAYER
by Frederick Seidel

But we are someone else. We're born that way.
The other one we are lives in a distant city.
People are walking down a street.
They pop umbrellas open when it starts to rain.
Some stand under an apartment building awning.
A doorman dashes out into the spring shower for
A taxi with its off-duty light on that hisses right past.
The daffodils are out on the avenue center strip.
The yellow cabs are yellow as the daffodils.
One exhausted driver, at the end of his ten-hour
    shift headed in,
Stops for the other one
We are who hides among the poor
And looks like the homeless out on the wet street
    corner.
Dear friend, get in.
I will take you where you're going for free.
Only a child's Crayola
Could color a taxi cab this yellow
In a distant city full of yellow flowers.

GOURDS
by Katharine S. White

ON MY SEED LIST THIS YEAR, THERE will be, as always, an item for one large packet of small ornamental (ovifera) gourds, in mixed colors and shapes. I don't know anything else I can buy for so little money that will give me so much pleasure from early June, when I drop the seed into the ground, until the following March, when I usually decide to discard, as too autumnal, the gourds I have harvested and polished in early October. Right now, there is a bowl of last fall's crop in the center of the dining table, and a group of ten or a dozen more gourds decorates the living-room mantelpiece. I never seem to tire of the compositions made by the colors and odd forms of these cousins of the squash: the smooth egg- or pear-shaped white ones, the sleek dark greens, which can be solid color or striped in self-color or white, the yellows, the oranges, the creams, the parti-colors—smooth and warted—and all in an interesting variety of shapes that change a little from year to year. Because I have waxed and polished them myself by hand, instead of buying those too shiny varnished gourds the florists sell, they have a lovely soft sheen, like the patina of old polished wood. Growing gourds is easy if you know a few small tricks. Plant them in full sun, and plant more than you want, in order to have a good selection of color and form. Plant them well away from your squashes, pumpkins, and melons, or there will be cross-pollination and you'll find, as we once did, an inedible monstrosity growing in your vegetable garden. The vines will need watering in dry spells, and the gourds must be covered at night when the first frosts come. When we let them ramble on the ground, we just throw some grain sacks over them on cold nights. When we grow them on a trellis, I cover each gourd at sundown with a paper bag. (There is no more pleasingly comic sight than a paper-bag vine.) Gourds are ready to harvest when the stem that holds the fruit to the vine is dry and snaps off easily. In our climate this moment is apt to come just as the World Series starts. Thus, about October 3, having picked and then washed each gourd with diluted rubbing alcohol, to kill the molds and viruses, and having coated each one with floor wax—paste wax, not liquid—I settle down peacefully to buff the gourds with a soft rag while I watch the ball games. It is perhaps my most relaxed moment in the year, combining as it does a sense of harvest with two of my favorite sports. All the big seed catalogues offer the mixed gourd seed, and I have had good luck with the mixtures I bought from Harris and Burpee. This year Breck's has a pleasing color picture of its De Luxe Mixture of small ornamentals and also offers a special variety called Aladdin, which is turban-shaped with red and yellow stripes. Park, the indefatigable, lists not only mixed seed but *eighteen* varieties of the small ovifera gourds, including one called the Ornamental Pomegranate, or Queen's Pocket melon, which the catalogue says is deliciously scented. I really must have that Queen's Pocket piece, and I trust that luck will bring me Willie McCovey and Willie Mays as well when I come to polish it. Possibly someone else would prefer to try one of Park's large gourds—those called lagenaria—say, the knobby Cave Man's Club, or the odd, swan-shaped Dolphin, or the Bombshell gourd, "a sensation when 1-in. Gourd-like fruit bursts forcibly."

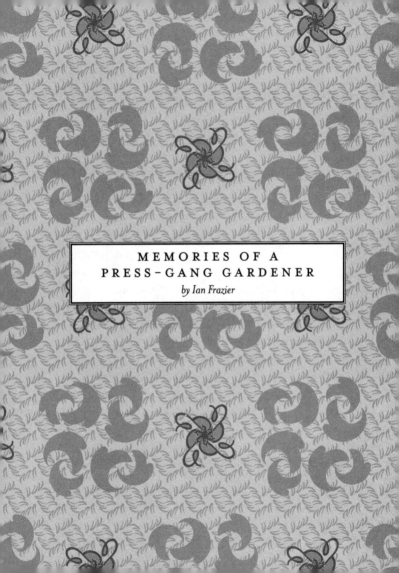

MEMORIES OF A
PRESS-GANG GARDENER

by Ian Frazier

MY FRIEND DONNIE'S MOTHER loved to garden. His house was just one house away from ours in the Midwestern suburb I grew up in—a short stroll down our lawn, across a street, up another lawn, and onto theirs. Donnie's mother had studied to be an opera singer in her youth, and she had a soaring alto voice which would come to us, disembodied, wherever in their house we happened to be: "Don-*EEEEeee!* Time-for-you-to-weed-the-*gaaaar*-den!" We dreaded the sound. Like most suburban boys of the 1960s, we were precocious cursers, and we stuffed the copies of *Playboy* magazine back under the bed and cursed our way out into the back yard. There, around the base of the trellises of the tea roses and at the edge of the strawberry patch, we pulled plantain weeds with a slowness that was exquisite and almost painful in how close it came to stopping without ever quite getting there.

Of course I could duck out and go to another friend's house, or even back to my own, but that would not necessarily save me from gardening

chores. The idea of a suburb was (and is) that a neighborhood should be a kind of park, with greenery flowing unbroken from one lawn to the next, decorated at regular intervals with ornamental plantings and obligatory shrubs. My family learned quickly that the suburban lawn requirement allowed for no exceptions. My father, perhaps only because he happened to own a scythe inherited from some forgotten farmer ancestor, planted our entire yard in rye one year. It came up tall and lush, head-high on the younger children, who loved to play in it. Then my father scythed it down, sweating in his T-shirt, really getting his back into it and leaving bucolic windrows, like a figure out of Winslow Homer, while the dads on lawns adjacent rode around on lawn tractors preening their yards to putting greens. The disapproval of the neighbors reached such a level that they might as well have marched to our doors in the middle of the night with torches and pitchforks. After a year or two of rye, Dad gave in and planted an acceptable lawn, to which my mother added a border of pachysandra next to the house. Usually pachysandra spreads

unstoppably, but ours, perhaps sensing it had been forced upon us, needed constant encouragement. "Weeding the pachysandra" was our house's dreaded job, a grim Devil's Island of a sentence which made helping in Donnie's mother's garden seem almost like fun, especially considering that there at least I had company.

My friend Kent, in the house diagonally across the street from ours, had less of a yard to deal with, but stricter parents. He labored under what seemed to me an appalling number of chores. Kent's mother had a thing for edging. She liked to keep the edges of the lawn bordering the driveway and the cement walk to the front door well trimmed and neat, a detail I was grateful my own parents overlooked. Kent or his brothers often did duty with a circular-blade edging tool, like a pizza cutter with a long handle, shaving micrometer-thin pieces of turf to give the driveway edges a ruled straightness that looked even more willed and crazy when compared to the unbarbered profusion of timothy grass and goldenrod growing in a between-yards weed patch not on their property just a few

feet away. Later Kent's family moved to a fancier house and his mother really went to town, putting in all kinds of pathways lined with railroad ties, and raised flower beds, and benches, and what we called her "cast-iron lawn poem"—an iron plaque on a stake, with a verse in raised letters painted white against a black background. The verse read:

The warmth of the sun for pardon,
The song of the birds for mirth;
One is nearer God's heart in a garden
Than anywhere else on earth.

As Kent sweated at stoop-labor among the railroad ties and I looked on from a lawn chair, enjoying a furtive beer—we were teenagers by then—the scorn we directed from time to time at that unoffending poem would have surprised its no doubt gentle author.

That anyone might garden voluntarily never seriously crossed any of us boys' minds. Gardening was something mothers and grandmothers did, an activity as alien to us as playing bridge or going to

the beauty parlor. But we did spend a lot of time outdoors fooling around, so our range and the gardeners' naturally overlapped. They would see us idling past and enlist us in one gardening job or another, and somehow we never found the strength of character to get away. In my family, my grandmother was the gardener whose press gang was hardest to avoid. She always had some new project in the works. When I was six and my second brother was being born, I stayed with her at her cottage on Lake Erie and immediately became the youngest member of a gardening crew that included her and a sixteen-year-old cousin. Grandmother could not believe that my parents had sent me out wearing only a flimsy pair of tennis shoes, and she commented on my parents' foolishness as I sat in a shoe store being fitted for a pair of black rubber overshoes. Then she led my cousin and me into a soggy woods enlivened with bursts of dogwood blooms, and we dug jack-in-the-pulpits and ferns and trilliums for replanting among the rocks on the lakefront bluff before her house. A few years later, after a cookout there, I invented a game which in-

volved floating paper plates next to the long concrete pier that ſtretched from Grandmother's
beach into the lake, and sinking the paper plates in
large ſplashes produced by a bombardment of those
same rock-garden ſtones. I had rîpped up a good
bît of the bluff before my father saw what I was doing and sat me down on the pier. He said that some
of those ſtones had been put there by my great-
grandmother fifty years before. Thinking about ît,
I ſtill feel guilty today.

But that was the problem at the center of our
basic unfittedness for gardening—we boys did not
want to husband and nurture and make things
grow, we wanted to deſtroy. Yes, we took some sat-
isfaćtion in looking back over the uniform smooth-
ness of a lawn we had juſt mowed, or at the
hand-textured brown of freshly weeded garden
earth. That didn't compare, though, to the deeply
pleasing rightness of walking a dîtchbank path wîth
a whîppy green ſtick in hand, beheading Queen
Anne's lace for a quarter of a mile at a ſtretch, then
turning to survey the long perſpećtive of whîte
blossoms tumbled on the ground or ſtaring down-

ward on partly severed stalks. I never did any
"turfing"—driving cars on golf courses at night and
spinning the rear wheels so as to dig tire marks in
the turf—but I admired the bold strokes left by the
latest turf artist on the fairways of the Lake Forest
Country Club, the brown double lines of tire tracks
extending in waves and curlicues across the green.
Putting boys like us to work in a garden was basically
a foxes-guarding-the-henhouse situation.

After my grandmother left the cold of Lake
Erie for permanent residence in Key West, Florida,
she continued to garden, and immediately fell in
with other lady gardeners there. Whenever I visited
she would find gardening work for me, often with a
friend of hers who would pay me a dollar or two an
hour. I once spent a long, hot morning thoroughly
weeding a flower patch for a woman named Natalie
Shein. At lunchtime, Natalie Shein came out on a
second-floor landing, surveyed my work from
above, and said, "You've pulled out all the aspi-
distras!" For a moment or two we regarded the
almost completely bare flower bed, the regularly
spaced holes where the flowers used to be, and the

torn-up blooms dying wiltingly on the pile of weeds I had made. I sat on the Bermuda grass below her, revealed once and for all as the vandal I truly was. Then, God bless her, Natalie Shein began to laugh. She laughed for a long time and then invited me in for lunch. We had conch salad and cold beer, and spent the rest of the afternoon at the kitchen table talking to two male friends of hers, a conversation the likes of which I had never heard before. I was seventeen years old, almost out of high school; my days as a press-gang gardener were done.

Donnie (now Don) and I are still friends. Though he grumbled as much as anyone on the gardening press gang, he grew up to be a gardener himself. He grows flowers, fruit trees, berry bushes, and vegetables in his yard in Portland, Oregon. He and I have been friends for forty-one years. I did not grow up to be a gardener, and as far as I know, neither did Kent. He and I haven't seen each other for a long time. In our twenties we used to go out and howl at the moon, as the expression is. We had both moved away from our hometown by

then, but we kept ending up back there a lot, sleeping late in our parents' houses and overstaying our welcome in general. One night we went to various taverns and to various friends' houses, and drove around on various back roads, and got home in the latest and darkest part of the night. The lights were still on at my house, and I stumbled in and went to bed. But at Kent's house the lights were out—not a good sign—and when he tried the back door it was locked. As he told me later, he went around trying the other doors; all were locked. In that neighborhood and in those days no one ever locked their doors. He had been deliberately locked out. He fumbled in the dark, looking for a window he could slide open, making noise. Then an urge overcame him and he stopped for a moment to attend to it. In the next second the outside lights all came on at once, and the back door flew open, and there stood his parents in pajamas and bathrobes. His mother gazed upon him and cried to his father, "Sam, he's urinating on my perennials!"

Ten minutes later, we were middle-aged. Kent's mother's words, which he and I made fa-

mous to each other, repeating them often as sort of a late-night party rallying cry, soon lapsed into disuse, and our friendship, too, expired. As I said, we have not been in touch for a long while. Don, on the other hand, I talked to on the telephone just a few days ago. He and I had gone fishing, and he arrived home to find all his tomato plants dead of a blight. I had tasted those tomatoes; they made me ashamed of the other tomatoes I had eaten in my life. Don was naturally concerned, and he went on about the possible causes of the blight and how he might do his garden differently next year. I enjoy listening to him and my other gardening friends talk about their gardens. I don't always follow very closely what they say, but I'm soothed, like an uncomprehending dog, simply by the sound. Art is long, and so is gardening; chaos and destruction have no appeal to me anymore. Now when I visit gardening friends, I sometimes drift out to the garden, ask what weeding needs to be done, and begin carefully to pull up cheeseflower and burdock unbidden, for no reason I can explain.

QUEEN-ANN'S-LACE
by William Carlos Williams

Her body is not so white as
anemone petals nor so smooth—nor
so remote a thing. It is a field
of the wild carrot taking
the field by force; the grass
does not raise above it.
Here is no question of whiteness,
white as can be, with a purple mole
at the center of each flower.
Each flower is a hand's span
of her whiteness. Wherever
his hand has lain there is
a tiny purple blemish. Each part
is a blossom under his touch
to which the fibers of her being
stem one by one, each to its end,
until the whole field is a
white desire, empty, a single stem,
a cluster, flower by flower,
a pious wish to whiteness gone over—
or nothing.

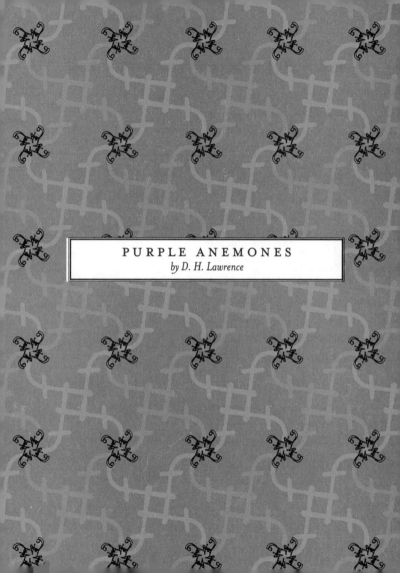

PURPLE ANEMONES
by D. H. Lawrence

Who gave us flowers?
Heaven? The white God?

Nonsense!
Up out of hell,
From Hades;
Infernal Dis!

Jesus the god of flowers——?
Not he.
Or sun-bright Apollo, him so musical?
Him neither.

Who then?
Say who.
Say it—and it is Pluto,

Dis,
The dark one.
Proserpine's master.

Who contradicts——?

When she broke forth from below,
Flowers came, hell-hounds on her heels.
Dis, the dark, the jealous god, the husband,
Flower-sumptuous-blooded.

Go then, he said.
And in Sicily, on the meadows of Enna,
She thought she had left him;
But opened around her purple anemones,

Caverns,
Little hells of colour, caves of darkness,
Hell, risen in pursuit of her; royal, sumptuous
Pit-falls.

All at her feet
Hell opening;
At her white ankles
Hell rearing its husband-splendid, serpent heads,
Hell-purple, to get at her—
Why did he let her go?
So he could track her down again, white victim.

Ah mastery!
Hell's husband-blossoms
Out on earth again.

Look out, Persephone!
You, Madame Ceres, mind yourself, the enemy is
    upon you.
About your feet spontaneous aconite,
Hell-glamorous, and purple husband-tyranny
Enveloping your late-enfranchised plains.

You thought your daughter had escaped?
No more stockings to darn for the flower-roots,
    down in hell?
But ah, my dear!
Aha, the stripe-cheeked whelps, whippet-slim
    crocuses,
At 'em, boys, at 'em!
Ho, golden-spaniel, sweet alert narcissus,
Smell 'em, smell 'em out!

Those two enfranchised women.

Somebody is coming!
Oho there!
Dark blue anemones!
Hell is up!
Hell on earth, and Dis within the depths!

Run, Persephone, he is after you already.

Why did he let her go?
To track her down;
All the sport of summer and spring, and flowers
    snapping at her ankles and catching her
    by the hair!
Poor Persephone and her rights for women.

Husband-snared hell-queen,
It is spring.

It is spring,
And pomp of husband-strategy on earth.

Ceres, kiss your girl, you think you've got her back.
The bit of husband-tilth she is,
Persephone!

Poor mothers-in-law!
They are always sold.

It is spring.

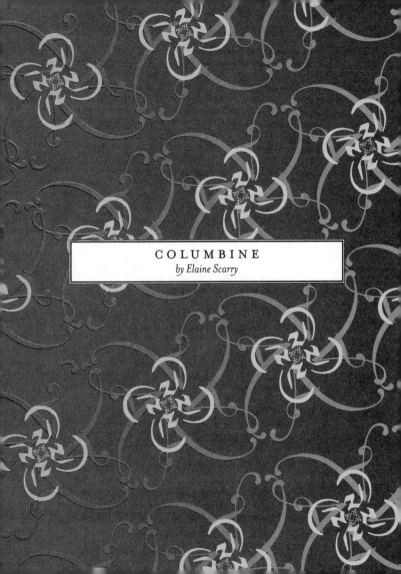

COLUMBINE
by Elaine Scarry

THE FIRST GARDEN I LIVED IN WAS very steep. The ground rose so steadily that if you were to enter from the front street and climb up the sequence of garden staircases to the dirt road at the top, you would have ascended to the height of a fourteen-story building.

The house in the garden was itself four stories high. But even to reach its front door you had first to climb up through a steep bank of lavender and blue phlox and then go up a second, briefer staircase that passed through a privet hedge and lifted you to the level of the morning glories by the front door. This second stairway was made of concrete and was walled in on either side to hold back the ground you were climbing through. At its bottom step, your head was below ground level; then, as you climbed, your eyes came level with the roots of the privet (which you were obliged to inspect for copperheads); then in another step or two you were safer, since it was no longer your face but only your shoulders, waist, legs that took their turn rising out of the ground.

From here the garden kept rising, sometimes in a sharp incline, sometimes by a wall where the ground level suddenly jumped, and running beside it were the walkways and staircases that lifted you up past pansies, lilies, columbine, hydrangea and iris, dahlias and zinnias, until the top, steepest staircase, which rose up beside the stalks of sunflowers, whose faces were exactly even with the ground of the upper road. From the road, you could watch the garden dropping back down into its deep well of color.

This steepness—this sense of life tilted on its side—belongs to all perennials, but above all to columbine. My garden is level now, but everywhere the columbine rises and flies, floats and falls, its blossoms turning up by my face, my feet, my waist, my thighs. I am steeped in them and can measure them against every part of me.

Their fluty colors—light pinks, light blues—mix with air and disappear into the sky like something that has flown too high to be identified. Uncertain bird: aquilegea-columbine. The tallest in the garden has blossoms that are three yellow shades: the petals are cornsilk, the spray of stamens the color of buttercups, and tawny spurs kick out behind. Each blossom looks like a shooting star itself shooting stamen-stars out in front and carrying four comets behind. Taller than I, its array of blossoms point up, point down, lift, dive, and dart away, their spurs curving under or arching out until the whole plant seems about to pitch and roll and wheel away. What keeps it trim, balanced, are the tiers of leaves stacked neatly below, like layers of mica or lace, or like the plumes of a dove when she ruffs her feathers and breaks the smooth surface into looping rows.

Steep flowers confound up and down, air and ground, as though there is no difference between being above and below. First perennial out of the earth, the columbine comes into the world fully formed. Not a shaft or a stem but a delicate curled ball of already lobed leaves, each layer perfect, lying inside the next, folded up like a nested staircase. It is as though no adjustment has been required. It is as though it had already leafed out underground, then packed up, arriving in the light like laughter (or a soft drumroll), ready to ruffle out in all directions.

This continuity between the below- and aboveground layers was in my first garden. The gardener was a coal miner and spent the first six hours of each day underground; then, after bathing, eating, and resting, he spent the afternoon working the earth from above. In summers, I would wake in mid-morning, climb up the garden stairways at noon, and walk along the top road watching for him; I stood at the hinge of his day. We would travel back to the garden together, dropping down all the garden staircases to the kitchen door, never cutting through the upper rooms of the house.

The gardener's boy had died when he was nine, and every four or five days we carried a basket of tall flowers to his grave. The cemetery (like everything in the town) was on the same steep incline as the garden, though it started one street lower on the mountainside, the graves proceeding downward like a grassy stairway counted off by the stone markers. The boy's grave was at the very bottom, but he was part of the high world, mixed in our minds with the tall flowers and only pressing on our attention in the late half of the day.

This confounding of up and down happened even when you were just walking inside the house. The doorsill on the bottom floor was at ground level; but as soon as you walked deeper into the room, the ground was already rising, so that soon you could see flower stems through the window, and at the backmost room there was no window at all, since you were now deep underground. There was no horizontal plane: just moving about already pitched you onto the vertical. The same was true on the second floor and the third: their front rooms hung suspended out into the air; their backmost rooms met the steep ground, so that you were always either traveling down or up, depending on whether you were moving toward the back or toward the front. The attic had side windows, equidistant from the ground; the front and back had closed-in eaves, which held the fragile objects the gardener had carried in the war.

The very steepness that ought to have made upper and lower distinct instead made the two interchangeable. In the steady roll of the earth, up and down somersault over and take one another's place. My first winter in the level garden, the plants all died. It was as though my hands, my eyes, my mouth had all been struck, bruised, and emptied. I had lost not just the things that had been sensed but the act of sensing itself. I cut up bright picture books, putting their colors everywhere on the walls, and tried to fill the windows with colored glass.

When the columbine came up, it was as though I was the first person on earth to see this happen. Only common sense restrained me from carrying the news all over town ("My garden, that died, has come back"). The airy cartwheel that carried it down out of view in November now carried it up in March. Trim soldier, at ease in its yearly spin, Columbine.

BIOGRAPHICAL NOTES

HILTON ALS is the author of *The Women*, recently published in paperback by The Noonday Press. He is currently at work on a novel.

TONY AVENT is the owner of Plant Delights Nursery in Raleigh, North Carolina, which features rare and unusual perennials, hostas, and U.S. Natives. He also owns the Juniper Level Botanical Gardens. As an international plant explorer, he travels widely and frequently. He has been the garden columnist at the *Raleigh News and Observer* since 1987, and he is a horticultural lecturer and consultant.

KAREL ČAPEK (1890–1938) was a Czech playwright, novelist, and essayist. He is best known for two brilliant satirical plays—*R.U.R.* (*Rossum's Universal Robots*), and *The Insect Play*, written with his brother Josef. "Buds" is from *The Gardener's Year*, first published in 1929.

GEOFFREY B. CHARLESWORTH's first garden was the backyard of a New York City brownstone,

where not even *Arabis caucasica* would grow. Years later, he started a five-acre garden in the Berkshires, and was soon the chair of the Connecticut chapter of the North American Rock Garden Society (NARGS). He later founded the Berkshire chapter with fellow gardener Norman Singer. He is the author of *The Opinionated Gardener* and *A Gardener Obsessed*, both published by David Godine. His main loves are the mountain and woodland plants of the U.S. West, the European Alps, and Turkey.

DAN CHIASSON is a poet working in Cambridge, Massachusetts. "Ovid at Tomi" is his first published poem.

HENRI COLE was born in Fukuoka, Japan, in 1956. He grew up in Virginia and graduated from the College of William and Mary. In 1995 he was the recipient of the Rome Prize in Literature from the American Academy of Arts and Letters. His fourth collection of poetry, *The Visible Man*, is forthcoming from Knopf. At present, he is Briggs-Copeland Lecturer in Poetry at Harvard.

COLETTE (1873–1954) was a French novelist and short-story writer. "Lily" and "Hellebore" are from *Flowers and Fruit* (1986), a collection of her writing on plants.

THOMAS C. COOPER is the editor of *Horticulture* magazine, the editor of numerous gardening books, and the author of *Odd Lots* (Henry Holt), a book of gardening essays. He lives and gardens on the outskirts of Boston.

KEN DRUSE is the award-winning author and photographer of fifteen books on gardening, including *The Natural Garden* (1989), *The Natural Shade Garden* (1992), and *The Natural Habitat Garden* (1994). He is the contributing garden editor to *House Beautiful* magazine, and is familiar to many gardeners from television appearances and lectures. In 1997 Druse's book *The Collector's Garden* received the Amer-

ican Horticultural Society's first award for Book of
the Year.

THOMAS FISCHER is executive editor of *Horticulture*, America's oldest gardening magazine. His
one-quarter-acre garden—best described as an on-
going experiment with unusual herbaceous and
woody plants—is in Boston. He has a particular
interest in hellebores, delphiniums, and other
members of the Ranunculaceae, and is always
attempting (with occasional unlikely successes) to
grow plants that are not supposed to be hardy in
southern New England. He is currently at work on
his first book.

MICHAEL FOX's work has appeared in *Raritan,
Prize Stories 1994: The O'Henry Awards,* and *Prism Interna-
tional.* He has an MFA from the University of
Michigan. He lives in Princeton, New Jersey.

IAN FRAZIER grew up in Hudson, Ohio, and at-
tended Harvard College. He was a staff writer for
The New Yorker for twenty-one years. He has pub-

lished several books of essays and two longer works of nonfiction, *Great Plains* and *Family*. In 1997 his collection of humor pieces *Coyote v. Acme* was awarded the first Thurber Prize for American Humor.

STEVEN A. FROWINE graduated from Ohio State with a degree in horticulture and received his master's degree from Cornell. With much experience in both the profit and nonprofit sides of gardening, he gives talks all over the United States and has written many articles for horticultural publications. In 1990, he joined White Flower Farm, one of the nation's top mail-order nurseries, where he served as vice president of horticulture. He recently started his own business, The Great Plant Company, whose mission is to bring discriminating gardeners the best and newest plants from all over the world.

NANCY GOODWIN's gardens at Montrose, in North Carolina, have been featured in a number of publications, including *House Beautiful*, *Horticulture*, and *The New York Times*. She was the founder and

owner of Montrose Nursery (1984–93), which originally specialized in cyclamen and also grew other little-known perennials and a few woody plants. Goodwin lectures across North America, and she has written many articles for books and journals. With Allen Lacy, she edited Elizabeth Lawrence's *A Rock Garden in the South*.

DANIEL HINKLEY, an avid plant person since youth, presently gardens on 7.5 acres on the North Kitsap Peninsula across the Puget Sound from Seattle, and with his partner, Robert Jones, operates a small mail-order nursery called Heronswood. His first book, *Winter Ornamentals*, was published in 1993, and he is currently working on *The Explorer's Garden: Unusual Perennials for American Gardens* for Timber Press. He travels frequently to Europe and Asia in search of new plants from nurseries as well as natural habitats.

MARY KEEN is an internationally published garden writer. She has written five books (all available in the United States). She also designs gardens for

private clients. Her most public commission was for the new opera house at Glyndebourne. Her own garden, in Gloucestershire, England, is regularly open to the public, and the making of it is featured in her most recent book, *Creating a Garden*. She is married, with four children and three grandchildren.

JAMAICA KINCAID's books include *At the Bottom of the River*, *Annie John*, *Lucy*, *A Small Place*, *The Autobiography of My Mother*, and *My Brother*. She is presently at work on her own book about gardening. She lives in Vermont.

MAXINE KUMIN's *Selected Poems 1960–1990* was published in 1997 by W. W. Norton, publishers also of her new poems, *Connecting the Dots*, and *Women, Animals and Vegetables: Essays and Stories*. She and her husband live on a farm in New Hampshire, where they raise horses and vegetables.

D. H. LAWRENCE (1885–1930) was one of the great novelists of the twentieth century. "Purple

Anemones" and "Sicilian Cyclamens" come from *The Complete Poems* (1964).

PHILIP LEVINE was born in 1928 in Detroit and was formally educated there, at the public schools and at Wayne University. After a succession of industrial jobs he left the city for good and lived in various parts of the country before settling in Fresno, California, where he taught at California State University until his retirement. He has received many awards for his books of poems, including the Lenore Marshall Award, the National Book Critics Circle Award, the National Book Award twice, and most recently the Pulitzer Prize for *The Simple Truth* (Alfred A. Knopf).

CHRISTOPHER LLOYD's parents bought the half-timbered manor house of Great Dixter in Great Britain in 1910: he was born there in 1921, and it remains his home today. He took control of the gardens in 1946. He has written more than a dozen books, including *The Well-Tempered Garden*, and

his latest, *Gardener Cook*, which has just been published by Frances Lincoln. He has been a regular columnist for the magazine *Country Life* since 1963, and he also writes for many other publications. The gardens at Great Dixter are open to the public.

DUANE MICHALS is a photographer who incorporates written text with his photographs. He lives in New York City but has also lived in upstate New York near Bennington, Vermont, where he has gardened for twenty-seven years. Recently he has had two new books published, *The Essential Duane Michals* and *Salute Walt Whitman*.

MICHAEL POLLAN gardens in Cornwall Bridge, Connecticut. He is the author of *Second Nature: A Gardener's Education* and *A Place of My Own: The Education of an Amateur Builder* (both available from Dell). He is an editor-at-large for *Harper's* magazine and a frequent contributor to *The New York Times*. He is currently working on a book about the changing relationship between plants and people.

DAVID RAFFELD is the author of three collections of poetry (most recently *Into the World of Men*, Adastra, 1997) and a verse play, *The Isaac Oratorio*. He is a frequent adjunct in the Departments of Religion and Philosophy at Williams College in Williamstown, Massachusetts, where he lives. He is also the editor of *Potlatcxh*, a journal of Arts and Science.

ELAINE SCARRY teaches at Harvard University, where she is the Cabot Professor of Aesthetics and General Theory of Value. Her writings include *The Body in Pain* and articles on war and the social contract. Her new book on the way images are formed in the mind will appear in spring 1999.

FREDERICK SEIDEL has won the Lamont Prize and the National Book Critics Circle Award in Poetry. His books include *Final Solutions*; *Sunrise*; *These Days*; *Poems, 1959–1979*; and *My Tokyo*. "Prayer" is from his most recent book, *Going Fast* (Farrar, Straus and Giroux, 1998).

GRAHAM STUART THOMAS is a noted horticulturist and the author and illustrator of several books. He has been awarded the Victoria Medal of Honour and the Veitch Memorial Medal by the Royal Horticultural Society, and the Dean Hale Medal of the Royal National Rose Society, and is a vice president of both societies. In 1975, he was awarded the Order of the British Empire for his work for the National Trust, to which he serves as Gardens Consultant.

F. KINGDON WARD (1885–1958) was an English plant collector, a geographer, and an author. He made many collecting expeditions, mostly to the remote borderlands of India, Burma, and China. "A Day on the Edge of the World" is from *Plant Hunting on the Edge of the World*.

MARINA WARNER is a novelist and critic who is presently a Fellow Commoner at Trinity College, Cambridge. *No Go the Bogeyman: Scaring, Lulling and Making Mock*, a study of fear, will be published by Farrar, Straus and Giroux in the fall of 1998.

KATHARINE S. WHITE was an editor at *The New Yorker* for thirty-four years. In 1958 she wrote the first of a series of fourteen garden pieces that appeared in *The New Yorker* over the next twelve years. The poet Marianne Moore originally persuaded White that these pieces would make a fine book, but it wasn't until after her death that her husband E. B. White assembled them for the collection *Onward and Upward in the Garden*.

WILLIAM CARLOS WILLIAMS (1883–1963) is regarded as one of the most important and original American poets of the twentieth century. He wrote "Queen-Ann's-Lace" in 1921.

ERNEST WILSON (1876–1930) was an English plant collector, botanist, and prolific writer. He traveled extensively all over the world, but particularly in China and Japan. "Honeypots and Silver Tree" is from *Smoke That Thunders*.

WAYNE WINTERROWD and his partner, Joe Eck, founded North Hill, a garden design firm, in

1977. Their seven-acre garden of the same name was the subject of a book they wrote together, *The Year at North Hill* (Little, Brown, 1995). Before becoming a garden consultant, Winterrowd taught for many years in public high schools in southern Vermont. He now travels extensively as a consultant and lecturer. He is a frequent contributor to *Horticulture* and other magazines, and the author of *Annuals for Connoisseurs* (Prentice Hall, 1992).

COLOPHON

The text of this book is set in Mrs. Eaves, a typeface created by Zuzana Licko of Emigre Fonts. Mrs. Eaves is a contemporary interpretation of Baskerville, a typeface designed by the English typographer John Baskerville in the mid-eighteenth century and named for Mrs. Eaves, his housekeeper. Licko has explored the idiosyncrasies of printing history and lavishly interpreted the anachronistic language of ligatures, creating a typeface of great legibility and character. The patterns in this book were designed using Hypnopædia and other custom pattern fonts also created by Zuzana Licko, and are rooted in the rich history of typographic ornamentation.

DESIGNED BY JESSICA HELFAND | WILLIAM DRENTTEL
WITH JEFFREY TYSON AND JUSTIN WOO
Falls Village, Connecticut